LOVING
LONGING
LEAVING

LOVING
LONGING
LEAVING

MICHAEL WELLER

THEATRE COMMUNICATIONS GROUP
NEW YORK
2011

Loving Longing Leaving is published by Theatre Communications Group, Inc., 520 Eighth Avenue, 24th Floor, New York, NY 10018-4156

This publication is made possible in part with public funds from the New York State Council on the Arts, a State Agency.

TCG books are exclusively distributed to the book trade by Consortium Book Sales and Distribution.

LIBRARY OF CONGRESS CATALOGING-IN-PUBLICATION DATA

Weller, Michael, 1942–
Loving longing leaving / by Michael Weller.—1st ed.
p. cm.
ISBN 978-1-55936-399-0
I. Title.
PS3573.E457L66   2011
812'.54—dc22   2011013338

Book design and composition by Lisa Govan
Cover design by Mark Melnick

First Edition, June 2011

For Kathy

CONTENTS

DO NOT DISTURB

Do Not Disturb (originally titled *What the Night Is For*) was first presented in 1999–2000, in a reading directed by Izzy Mant at the Criterion Theatre as one of a series of workshops produced by Theatre Machine and supported by Act.

Do Not Disturb (originally titled *What the Night Is For*) received its world premiere on November 27, 2002, at the Comedy Theatre in London's West End. It was directed by John Caird; the design was by Tim Hatley, the lighting design was by Paul Pyant, the sound design was by Rich Walsh. The cast was:

LINDY METZ   Gillian Anderson
ADAM PENZIUS   Roger Allam

Do Not Disturb (originally titled *What the Night Is For*) received its American premiere on April 3, 2004, at the Laguna Playhouse (Andrew Barnicle, Artistic Director; Richard Stein, Executive Director) in Laguna Beach, CA. It was directed by Richard Stein; the scenic and costume design were by Dwight Richard Odle, the lighting design was by Tom Ruzika, the sound design was by David Edwards; the production stage manager was Rebecca Green. The cast was:

LINDY METZ	Claudia Christian
ADAM PENZIUS	Kip Gilman

CHARACTERS

MELINDA (LINDY) METZ, a teacher of Special Education, late thirties to early forties

ADAM PENZIUS, an architect, late thirties to early forties

PLACE

A hotel in a Midwestern town.

TIME

Recently.

NOTE

A " / " in dialogue indicates when one thought is dropped suddenly and another intercrossing thought, or alternate formulation of the idea, continues without transition.

SCENE 1

Darkness. Pop—a champagne cork! Laughter.

Lights up on a hotel room decorated in a bland, traditional style. We could be in any of the better chain hotels in a mid-sized Midwestern city.

Lindy and Adam sit at a table eating a meal off a trolley with silver domes. A hanging fixture over the table closes them in a tight embrace of light. Another lamp on one side of the double bed is on low beside a digital alarm-radio.

Lindy is full-figured with soft features. Her voice is quietly cadenced but she has sudden bursts of infectious mirth. She wears a tastefully stylish suit. Adam has thinning hair and an easy but, at times, brisk efficient manner; a man used to giving orders. He's in tie and shirtsleeves, jacket flung on the bed.

The mood is upbeat but a little shrill, each trying too hard to act relaxed.

LINDY *(Guessing)*: Millman? Hillman? Spillman? Spellman?

ADAM: No.

LINDY: Don't tell me, don't—*Gell*man. It was *Gellman*, right?

ADAM *(Enjoying this)*: Nope.

LINDY: He was an ear-nose-and-throat man—

ADAM: Yes—

LINDY: With a hideous wife—

ADAM: Yes—

LINDY: Isn't she the one who got drunk once and said we should skip the book discussion and try group sex for a change?

ADAM: That's the one.

LINDY: His name was Gellman, I'm sure it was. That week was *Bonfire of the Vanities*.

ADAM: Right book, wrong doctor. Gasarch. Dr. Gasarch.

LINDY: You know, I think you're right. He tried to grope me in the hallway my first night in the Book Circle. Well, doctors tend to be pretty biological on the whole. Don't you find?

ADAM *(Absurdly)*: On the whole, absolutely.

LINDY *(Giggles)*: Do you still see any of that bunch—

ADAM: The Get-a-Life Culture Club?

LINDY: Were they that pathetic?

ADAM: Present company excepted.

LINDY: Thank you.

ADAM: Actually, I did run into—was that obstetrics guy before your time, Dr. Nicklaus?—vacation in Bora Bora at one of those, what are they, along the beach, open-side-thatched-roof-bar-type things. He introduced me to a little dark-haired cutie-pie young enough to be someone he just delivered. His wife, he called her. The only good joke he ever told.

(Lindy raises her champagne glass.)

LINDY: A toast: To the Book Circle.

ADAM: And all that came of it! *(They click glasses)* Tattinger. You remembered.

LINDY: I did? Oh . . . *(Then)* Remembered what?

ADAM: My favorite champagne.

LINDY: It's the little touches that do a perfect hostess make.

ADAM: You *didn't* remember?

LINDY: I'm sure I did. Sub-thing-a-mally. You've barely touched your fish.

ADAM: Ditto your meat.

(They take bites with awkward movements.)

LINDY: How is it?

ADAM: My fish is fine. How's your meat?

LINDY: Good, actually. Quite succulent and, um— tender— *(Hearing innuendo)* Oh dear, oh dear, Adam Penzius!

ADAM: Your nose still turns red when you blush.

LINDY *(Busying herself with food)*: So tell me all about yourself. How's your—you know, everything, life. You talk while *I* eat, then we'll switch 'round and I'll provide the ambient sound while you tackle your fish. How's that for a plan?

ADAM: You haven't changed, Lindy.

LINDY: It's a little warm though, isn't it? The hotel said they're testing a new air-conditioning system . . . I'll open a window, why don't I do that, I'll just— Aren't you warm? Aren't I babbling?

ADAM: I guess we're nervous.

LINDY: A little.

ADAM: Understandably.

LINDY: I'll just / It *is* warm . . .

(She goes to the window. Adam rises.)

—A boy was it? How old?

(Adam almost calls her on this, testing her memory, but then takes his jacket from the bed and removes some photos. She turns. They're awkwardly close together.)

ADAM *(Showing her a photo)*: Roo.
LINDY: Roo? For Rudolf?
ADAM: For Roo. As in "Kanga and——" From *Winnie the Pooh.* He curls up in my lap at breakfast, snuggles under my bathrobe like a baby kangaroo.
LINDY: He's ten?
ADAM: Clinging to his youth. Greg's his name; Gregory.

(They are inches apart, Lindy feels a wave of something and moves back to the table.)

What were yours again?
LINDY: Same as before: Doug and Willy.
ADAM *(Manly voice)*: That's right: "The Guys."

(He returns to the table with his photos and sits.)

LINDY: They are that, regular little jocks. Not so little now. Not completely jock, either, though Hugh does his best to push them that way. Football, baseball, basketball, anything with balls. *La Maison Testosterone,* that's what I call home. Is that your wife in the doorway?

(He looks puzzled and half turns toward the door behind him. Lindy grins, eyeing the photo.)

In the picture.

(Adam looks at the photo.)

ADAM *(Surprised)*: Oh, yes. Yes, that's——yes.

LINDY: What's *she* like?

(He studies the picture, sets it aside.)

ADAM: Oh, she's / she went back to work.
LINDY: That's what she's *like?*
ADAM: No, I mean— Career happens to be her focus right now, is all I— *[meant]* —When you asked . . .

(He lifts the photo again, glances at it, puts it down, then brings the photos back to his coat on the bed to put them away, all with abstracted movements, mind and body running separately . . .)

She earned a break after all those years full-time-momming it. You lose momentum in the job market, dancers especially, well, women in general—which is why she ended up starting her own business. It's an incredible amount of work, but it's finally paying off. Direct marketing, that's her— *[field]* / Selling lists of buyers to various sellers. Interested in finding buyers. To sell to. So, anyway. Yeah, she travels a lot.

(He sits back at the table. Lindy sets down her napkin.)

LINDY: And you're home with Greg?
ADAM: I really love being with him. Almost more than anything.
LINDY: I never thought you'd marry—"Jan," was it?
ADAM: Why not?
LINDY: Living together all that time, six years?
ADAM: Nine-ish. Actually.
LINDY: Could be seen as a sign of, oh, ambivalence?
ADAM: More a sign of the times; priorities, other things first.

LINDY: Well, Adam. Quite the snazzy life you lead. Traveling architect. With traveling wife. Each with their own business, his and hers, just like towels. Plus a cute little boy. *(Beat)* A nanny?

ADAM: Of course. *(Playing her game)* And a brownstone, a summer place in Kent, Connecticut, all the trimmings.

LINDY: Sounds . . . nice.

ADAM: It is, actually. It's really nice.

LINDY: Well . . . good.

ADAM: And you?

LINDY *(Shrugs)*: Oh-blah-dee, life goes on. More bubbly?

(Both start to rise.)

ADAM: *I'll* pour.

LINDY: My hotel room, you're the guest. *(She pours for them both)* Actually, I *like* playing hostess. Trained from girlhood, you know. Cranbrook Juniors. All us marriageable gals were sent there to master etiquette and comportment, not to mention home ec and floral arrangement. The essentials.

ADAM: I never pegged you as the hostess type. The way you were in New York I'd have thought—

LINDY: New York was a parentheses. Before and after is the real me.

ADAM: What's tonight; parentheses, or real?

LINDY: Tonight— *(She stops; blushing)* Well. You called. Cheers.

(They clink glasses across the table.)

ADAM: So, are there Book Circles out here?

LINDY: In the Midwest, you mean? You'd be surprised by the amenities "out here." We have electricity, supermarkets, copycat crime . . .

ADAM: I didn't mean it that way. *(Sees her smile)* Like some condescending New York asshole.

LINDY: Should I order a second bottle?

ADAM: You're so damn lovely. *(Then)* Sorry.

(He looks down, abashed.)

LINDY: You've held up pretty well yourself.

(The sudden attraction overwhelms them both.)

(Quick, sing-song) Is that fold-out sofa still in the conference room?

ADAM *(Welcoming the change of pace)*: The client couch? The Famous Aztec Hippie Folding Futon?

LINDY: God, wasn't it hideous. Did your wife choose it?

ADAM: My wife?

LINDY: No one with taste would've picked something like that so I figured it must be a concession to family. Or a charitable gesture to the sight impaired.

ADAM: My *partner's* wife, in fact. During her "liberated" phase. She threatened to leave him, so he "recognized her aesthetic professional dimension" by putting her on salary as an interior design consultant. The sofa's long gone.

LINDY: And the wife?

ADAM: Also gone; Key West, lives with a janitor on a houseboat! *(Shakes his head in wonderment, backing himself into a world of feelings bigger than he's ready for)* Life!

LINDY: Oh-blah-dee. I was surprised to hear from you.

ADAM *(Okay, time to deal with it)*: It never crossed your mind I might one day . . . ?

LINDY: Why *now*? What made you— *(She stops)*

ADAM: A job was taking me near your neck of the woods / seemed like a chance to catch up.

LINDY: After ten years?

ADAM *(With a slight edge)*: Well, it wasn't *me* who upped and left New York without a word— *(Stops)* I never knew for sure if you'd want to hear from me.

LINDY *(Composing herself to answer)*: I apologize. It *was* abrupt, yes. Things sort of *erupted* one day; Hugh's dad, him racing back here for the funeral, to run the company. And I had the whole family to pack, the kids. Not to mention ready myself to meet the Metz clan for the first time. It was . . . chaos.

ADAM: It would have helped to know that.

LINDY: Of course. I acted thoughtlessly. The Cranbrook Juniors Academy would not approve of how I handled our / actually, I don't think / *is* there an established etiquette for ending a fling?

ADAM *(Irritated)*: Fling?

LINDY *(Conceding)*: Okay, "affair"?

ADAM: Is that what it was?

LINDY: When a married woman with two young children and a married man—well, *almost* married, cohabiting for nine-ish years—*Jan* is it?

ADAM *(Cutting through)*: You know perfectly well.

LINDY *(Quickly)*: When you meet in secret after Book Circle and end up naked and sweaty on a futon in his office-loft for hours and hours, isn't that exactly the meaning of, yes, "affair." *(Then)* "Torrid affair"? Is that better?

ADAM: Your nose is red.

LINDY *(Smiling)*: You're getting a meal out of my guilt. And the food here isn't cheap, believe me.

ADAM: And we *are* in your room.

LINDY: I should explain that—

ADAM: No need . . .

LINDY: I'm expecting a call.

ADAM: From your husband?

LINDY *(Hesitating)*: No, actually . . . from Keeshon.

ADAM: Should I know that name?

LINDY: He's just a kid— *(Then)* No, actually he's an *amazing* kid. He was drawing on the sidewalk one day, you know, chalk; this huge picture of a baby with a red blob where the head should be. I asked him why the head was that color: "It's his mouff wide open crying blood 'cause he alone." So I gave him a few dollars to draw me some pictures . . . food money, really. He's homeless. Eleven years old. Dad shot him in the chest for crying too loud when he was five. Anyway, it all got out of hand . . . he called me one night from jail and I had to arrange for his release. Since then I've become his safety net. And I don't know how to get out of it, I can't just walk away / well, I could— *(She stops)*

ADAM *(Lightly)*: And so here we are, in your room.

LINDY: If you saw his work you'd understand . . . He's a natural artist, goes right to the heart of it.

ADAM: Lindy, you don't have to explain yourself.

LINDY: Anyway, nights are hard for him, so he calls me if he needs to talk. And I'm out of town for the weekend, so . . . I gave him my number at the hotel.

ADAM: Okay. *That's* why we're here.

LINDY: Yes, Adam, that's why we're here.

ADAM *(Pushing it)*: And the cell phone in your purse? You couldn't have given him *that* number? In case you wanted to dine out with me? Instead of in?

LINDY *(Caught)*: If I said it was broken, would you check?

ADAM: I'd wonder why the elaborate excuse for wanting to be alone with me?

LINDY *(After thinking a moment, she decides to level with him)*: All right. Damn you, Adam. My family . . . my husband's family, they're . . . *prominent.* Metz Bicycles, you know— after Schwinn, what else *is* there? And Hugo's weighing a run for Congress—and so, if Mrs. Metz was seen dining with a strange man several hundred miles from home, a man not part of the education conference here . . . and word got back, which it definitely would, this is a very very when-you-boil-it-down small state . . . I'd have to explain "the interesting-looking man I had dinner with last Saturday," and I'd get another lecture about political enemies looking for any hint of impropriety, etc., etc. . . . I don't lie very well, I'm afraid; this darn nose.

ADAM: Why lie about having dinner with an old friend?

LINDY: Let's change the subject.

ADAM: What'd you to tell him back in New York?

LINDY: That I was with devoted readers discussing books.

ADAM: Till two in the morning?

LINDY: He trusted me. *(She has revealed too much)*

ADAM *(Picking up on it immediately)*: Trus*ted*?!

LINDY: Don't go there, Adam. *(Brighter, a little too much energy)* Does your boy ever say that? "Hey, Doug, got a new girlfriend?" "Don't go there, Mom." Oh, and "snap." Everything cool is "snap" now. Has that caught on back east? Or is it already old.

ADAM: My boy's still in the "Butt-Brain" phase: Vomit-Breath. Penis-Head. Doo-Doo-Face.

LINDY: Oh god, I *adored* that age, it was so, so *noisy* and *physical* and honest, isn't that what always goes on between people just under the surface—my husband watches C-SPAN, all these stuff-shirt politicos—"I object to the suggestion of my esteemed colleague from Texas," meaning, "Liar, liar, pants on fire," or, "I'm morally opposed to the notion that—" when what they really *mean* is, "Up yours, Butt-Brain!" *(Realizing she has become too animated, she backpedals)* One often feels.

(She grows quiet, sips champagne, then bursts out laughing at herself.)

ADAM: *This* is how I remember you. Irreverent and breathless and blurting out anything that came to your mind. You

seem so subdued tonight. Are you being *careful* with me?
Or is this the before-and-after-New-York Lindy?

LINDY *(Beat)*: Eat your fish.

ADAM: No, let's *not* change the subject.

(After a silence, the alarm-radio clicks on, filling the room with deafening music.)

LINDY: Damn it, for two days that thing's been . . . excuse me.

(She tries to turn it off, jiggling buttons, poking them, standing mystified.)

How do I stop it?!

(She pokes more buttons. Adam stands beside her, leaning toward the gizmo.)

ADAM: This one on the end works the alarm.

(He lowers the volume. It's a moody blues. They straighten inches apart. The intimacy is inescapable.)

Did we ever dance?

LINDY: We skipped the preliminaries. If memory serves.

(They stand like this for a moment.)

ADAM: Never too late.

(Lindy turns off the radio.)

LINDY: I think I need a clearer idea of what's going on here before—more goes on.

ADAM *(Flirting)*: We're having dinner. In your room. Because your nose might give you away if you tried explaining me to your husband. Who doesn't trust you like he used to.

(Both burst out laughing at what is so clearly near the surface.)

LINDY *(Covering her nose shyly)*: Is it *very* red?
ADAM: Extremely.

(Lindy grows animated, nervous, absently rearranging things on the table.)

LINDY: Why aren't you *different*, Adam! Why don't you have a pot belly and, and you know, be irritable and wear thick glasses or something. Like this couple at my high school reunion, the husband you could smell his cheap aftershave across the room, and his shoulders were white with dandruff, he was all swollen-looking with this swollen wifey-person in a peach-coralish gown, an inflated Mid-Life-Ken and Barbie and/but there was something about him, I don't know, he reminded me of *you*.
ADAM: Thank you so much.
LINDY: Maybe Adam looks like that, I thought. Swelling up, puffy and old. Which would make our whole episode, you know . . . easier to let go—

(She is still fussing, not looking at him.)

And then you called and your voice sounded the same, and—well, that can happen, voices stay young while the rest sags and droops . . .

(She's still. She doesn't look at him.)

I never expected . . . When you walked in—!

ADAM: Me, neither. I thought you'd be—

LINDY: No, I mean, Adam, you haven't changed is the thing. At all.

ADAM: And you're perfect.

LINDY *(Shy)*: Yeah, right . . .

ADAM: When the door opened I thought: "This is what she was growing towards. Now she's perfect."

(They stare at each other lost in possibilities. Lindy turns away.)

LINDY: How do things get so intense around you so very fast? You'd think after all this time . . . *(She fans herself, comically relieving heat)* I mean—*whew*! *(Brighter)* So, how long are you in town for? Did you say?

ADAM: I leave tomorrow night.

LINDY: Business.

ADAM: A client. Potential. If he approves my bid after the final presentation tomorrow. Which he will.

LINDY: He said quivering with self-doubt.

ADAM: I'm much in demand.

LINDY: So you just—decided to look me up?

ADAM *(Avoids answering directly)*: More or less. This job's not my usual kind of bid: "Environmentally Responsible Office Blocks of Visual Distinction," meaning "not too high and lots of trees." But it's easy money, the work is A-B-C stuff, my assistants can handle most of it, so I figured I could buy a little freedom to polish a few projects for international competition.

LINDY: Good luck.

ADAM: Thank you.

(The veil of small talk is wearing thin.)

LINDY *(Not ready for the next step)*: Shall we toast your what-is-it, final sales pitch?

(She pours more champagne.)

ADAM *(Slightly huffy)*: "Presentation." It's called a—
LINDY: "Presentation," sorry.
ADAM *(Carefully)*: If I nail it, I'll have to make trips out here pretty often.
LINDY: Poor Adam. Mind you, there *are* diversions to be had. Just a stone's throw down the pike there's the celebrated Candy Bar Museum of North America, featuring the largest gumdrop in the world. It weighs several hundred pounds, they say. There's even a gift shop with miniature Gummy Bear rings available nowhere else in the known universe.
ADAM: I was thinking more along the lines / maybe we could say hello from time to time.
LINDY: "Hello"?
ADAM: Have lunch together.
LINDY: I don't live here, Adam, I'm attending a conference. Home is two hundred miles away.
ADAM: A short hop.
LINDY *(A teasing smile)*: Two hundred miles? For lunch?
ADAM: Why not, if you were free.
LINDY: Neither of us is free.
ADAM: You know what I mean.
LINDY: Yes, and so on.

(They sip and think for a moment.)

ADAM: How early do you leave tomorrow?
LINDY: Seven A.M. US Air.

ADAM: There's nothing later? My final meeting's not till three. We could have—brunch.

LINDY: We have tonight.

ADAM: I see.

LINDY: Your food's getting cold.

ADAM: I'm not hungry.

LINDY *(Suddenly lighter)*: Before I forget!

(She brings him a tiny gift box from a shopping bag.)

ADAM: What's the occasion?

LINDY: Just a Goofy Gift.

(He holds the box, smiling at the memory.)

ADAM: Oh my god. I've kept them all, you know, the ceramic shopping bag, the miniature abacus, the sailboat mobile—

LINDY *(Breaking in)*: Open it.

(Adam opens the box and unwraps lavender tissue paper: a tiny, wooden, bendable cow.)

ADAM *(Bewildered)*: A small . . . wooden . . . cow?

LINDY: Local folk art. Push the button underneath.

(Adam holds it up and pushes. The cow collapses.)

(Comical cow voice) "My knees are weak!" *(He pushes again)* "Mooo!!!"

ADAM: They always had a secret meaning, your Goofy Gifts. That ceramic paper bag, wasn't that to—

LINDY: —To hold our secrets.

ADAM: And the abacus was to keep track of how many times—

LINDY: —In one night.

ADAM: What was the sailboat mobile, something about—?

LINDY: "Into the sunset. Happy endings."

ADAM: Of course, how could I forget. So this would be . . . ?
(Pushes the button idly under the cow)

LINDY *(In playful response)*: "My knees, my kneeeeees!!!"

ADAM *(Thinking)*: I push a button underneath and . . . *(Onto something)* Ah, her knees grow weak. Am I warm?

LINDY *(Flirting outrageously now)*: *I* am.

ADAM: Why a cow?

LINDY: They were sold out of the wife-and-mother adulterer models.

ADAM *(Still unsure)*: Is the Goofy Gift for old time's sake? Or is it more a present tense kind of deal?

LINDY: Yes.

ADAM: Yes, *which?*

LINDY *(Smiles)*: "Moooo."

ADAM: I'm assuming it's all right if I kiss you?

LINDY: Or we could talk about a book first, if that would help you relax. *(Teasing)* Read anything good lately?

ADAM: I just want to be sure.

(She smoothes her dress. They approach shyly, teenagers with a first kiss. As they start to embrace, the alarm-radio goes off at deafening volume.)

Damn it.

LINDY: Didn't you turn it off?

ADAM: I thought so.

(He finds a button that makes it quieter by degrees. Then he turns to her. They approach each other about to dance when the telephone rings.)

LINDY: Oh, shit—Keeshon. I forgot. The music.

(Adam switches off the alarm-radio.)

ADAM: Do you want privacy? Should I go in the / somewhere?
Bathroom?

*(She signals "stay," and picks up the phone. Adam crosses
the room, giving her privacy.)*

LINDY: Hello? *(Surprised by the voice she hears)* Oh . . . Hugh,
I— No, I was in the middle of—I was just eating
dinner. —I didn't feel like going out, it's been a long
day. —Very interesting so far . . . some unscheduled
speakers . . . They talked about their field of expertise,
darling, it's technical—

(She seems a little irritated.)

Has Doug done his homework? —A make-up game
tomorrow is no excuse, he has to finish the paper *tonight*—
Football isn't going to make him more sociable, he's a
private person, he's *thoughtful*, and playing mediocre
football doesn't make him feel better about himself—

*(She takes her near-empty champagne glass from the table.
The subject has been changed.)*

It's on top of the— Why does he need a laxative, are you
feeding him junk food? —Look in the medicine cabinet,
top shelf. —And what about the casserole I left in the
freezer, didn't you have it for dinner? —Pizza!!?? No
wonder he's constipated!

*(She looks apologetic for dragging Adam through this
mundane domesticity. Adam's raised eyebrows make her
grin.)*

Is Willy there? Okay, when they get home give them a hug for me . . . a *manly* football hug.

(She drains her champagne.)

Well, actually, Hugh, I was thinking—there's a few elective sessions tomorrow / not part of the main conference, but the subjects interest me and I'd like to attend. There's an extra flight Sundays at— *(Referring to nothing)* Let's see, 4:35, I could—

(Adam notes her "act," and her almost-empty champagne glass. While she speaks, he brings over the bottle and tips it. It is almost empty, so he pours his own champagne into her glass, an intimate gesture . . .)

Yes, I realize you'd miss your golf, for once in eleven years, but these are people whose work I should know better— *Who are they?* Specialists, Hugh, you wouldn't know them— Dr. Anna Weiss and Jacobo Boyle. —Hugh . . . I won't beg permission to stay an extra day, *part* of a day, actually— Well, it feels like begging— *(More outburst than she intended)*

Thank you. —Remember, thaw the casserole before the football game. —There's a note on top how to cook it. —Me, too. Good night.

(She hangs up. The game with the champagne has created a closeness between them.)

(Hand over nose) It must be glowing in the dark.
ADAM: Anna Weiss and Jacobo—?
LINDY: *Boyle.* They're real. I could never make up names like that. Yes, I could. *(Then)* The seminars are real.

ADAM: I thought you planned to leave in the morning.

LINDY: I did.

ADAM: Why memorize tomorrow's events?

LINDY (*Silly question*): As my son would say: "Duh!"

ADAM: Will Hugh check your story?

LINDY: He already has, I bet. I left a conference schedule under some paperwork on my desk. He found it, felt clever and relieved, and right about now he'll be starting to feel a little guilty that he didn't trust me.

ADAM: Your deceitfulness is impressively thorough.

LINDY: Thank you, and yours? If *your* wife calls your hotel and you're . . . elsewhere?

ADAM: Why would she call?

LINDY: To say hello? Ask where you left the oatmeal soap? I don't know, married stuff? She could just get lonely and feel like talking.

ADAM: She doesn't get lonely.

LINDY: *Everyone* gets lonely.

ADAM: Some people don't know that's what it is. They don't call. They—work.

LINDY: What if there's an emergency at home?

ADAM: Are you getting cold feet?

LINDY: I'm being careful, Adam. New York was playing with matches. Now it's a big bonfire we have to watch out for, two families and all.

ADAM (*Lifting his jacket*): Beeper. I'm a dial tone away. (*He moves to her. She turns away*) What's wrong?

LINDY: I don't know. Something feels . . . odd.

ADAM: Unfamiliar? Ten years.

LINDY: No, I mean . . . What do I mean? I could always feel your moods. You seem . . . hesitant. (*Then*) When you bid on the job here, did you know I lived nearby?

ADAM (*Seemingly perplexed*): That's a strange question.

LINDY: Did you?

ADAM: Why?

LINDY *(Working it out)*: If you knew how close to here I lived—and, I mean, you talked like this client wasn't your usual kind of suspect, so I'm wondering if you're after it for purely professional reasons or if I have something to do with, yes, that's what I mean, I'm worried that you *need* something you're not saying, something from me. Do you?

ADAM *(Too casually)*: My secretary screwed up the hotel reservation so I went online to check the booking and—there it was, Metz Bicycles, on the website, a pop-up with moving wheels . . .

LINDY: Yes, I know the logo, thank you.

ADAM: I put two and two together. Metz, of Lindy fame. You never said much about your personal life, but I remembered some mention of "Hugo's Bicycle Fortune." I did a search. Bingo.

LINDY: You just stumbled across my name.

ADAM: Pure accident.

LINDY: No hidden agenda.

ADAM: Plain old curiosity: how's she doing, what's she like now?

LINDY: Your once-upon-a-time mistress?

ADAM: We did have fun. Weren't you a little curious all these years? Isn't that why you're here?

LINDY: Actually . . . I came to get laid.

ADAM *(Beat)*: Well. That's *(What?)* —clear.

LINDY: Only that, Adam. Nothing more.

ADAM: Just like old times.

LINDY *(Picks up the phone, watching Adam)*: This is room 410. Hold my calls for tonight. Thank you. *(She hangs up)* *(She smiles, offering lightly)* "Moo"?

(The lights dim.)

SCENE 2

A while later. Lindy and Adam sit apart, she is in an armchair facing away from him, he is on the bed watching her. Both are disheveled, flushed and disoriented.

LINDY: What a mistake!
ADAM: Which part?
LINDY: Taking your call, meeting you, everything, everything!

(He watches her. The room is quiet.)

Don't look at me.
ADAM: You're breathtaking.
LINDY: I'm a mess.
ADAM: You're in disarray.
LINDY: No, Adam, I'm a mess. Sorry about this.

(Silence.)

ADAM: That was some curveball: "I came to get laid."

LINDY: Oh, yes, trying to slip back in the old groove: "A Walk on the Wild Side with Lindy Metz."

ADAM: What just happened?

LINDY: You mean "happened twice in rapid succession." With my clothes still on!

ADAM: Really?

LINDY: And nothing for you, poor Adam.

ADAM: At least one of us had fun. Twice.

LINDY: And I thought down there was all sort of . . . dead.

ADAM: Just sleeping?

LINDY: Yes. Like Sleeping Beauty, one kiss in the right place . . . *(Brighter)* Maybe that's what that story's about, *all* fairy tales in fact, maybe they're about sexual awakening, sort of toddler versions of sex to plant a seed for later, when we're ready for the real thing.

ADAM: Lindy, anything that pops into your head right now's going to seem erotic.

(She shivers with pleasurable memory.)

LINDY: I mean, Sleeping Beauty; it's so *blatantly* sexual— here comes Sir Knight on his milky white stallion: "Oh, look who's lying there on her back, waiting to be kissed, I bet if I pressed my knightly mouth against her soft lips, that little filly would buck and tremble right to life." I mean, please. There's a book about this, right? Must be. *(Genuinely intoxicated by this idea) Sex and the Fairy Tale.* Someone's already thought of it.

ADAM: I'll ask at the next Book Circle.

LINDY *(Caught)*: Oh. Am I trying to . . . ? —Yes I am / change the subject. I *am* sorry about all this, Adam.

ADAM: Never apologize for what happens between us.

(His focus is intense. She stands abruptly.)

LINDY (*Speaking with too much animation*): How would you like some ice water?

ADAM: There's nothing I'd like less.

LINDY: We can't sit around here for the rest of the night leaking. (*Mock hearty*) We have to get hold of ourselves!

ADAM (*Amused*): "*Get hold* of ourselves"?

LINDY: Ice water's actually a very good way to—

ADAM: Put a chill on things.

LINDY: In fact.

ADAM: Fine. Ice water.

(*Lindy goes into the bathroom. Adam places a pillow over his crotch, tries to change his thoughts. Lindy speaks from the bathroom, accompanied by sounds of running water.*)

LINDY (*From off*): Everything okay out there?

ADAM: Everything's hunky-dory.

LINDY (*From off*): No swelling?

ADAM (*Baffled*): Swelling?!

LINDY (*From off*): From—having to stop prematurely?

ADAM: Why would there be . . . ? What are you *talking* about?!

LINDY (*From off*): That *thing* that happens when men have to stop before they, um . . . Hugh said it's like a clogged drain that backs up and you swell—down there. It's very painful he says: "pink balls," something like that?

(*Adam shakes his head in disbelief, not sure she's putting him on.*)

ADAM: "Blue balls"?

LINDY (*From off, laughing*): Blue, that's right! I had this picture when he told me—little blueberries exploding on a bush. You don't have that, do you?

ADAM: My blueberries are fine, thank you.

(Lindy stands in the doorway holding two glasses of water. She has fixed herself up again. With her hair down and suit jacket off, and the light from the bathroom framing her, she looks achingly sensual.)

LINDY: That was a close call.

ADAM *(Smitten)*: Lindy!

LINDY *(Cutting him short)*: Ice?

(She goes to the ice bucket, puts the glasses down. Adam tries to recover his equilibrium.)

ADAM: So, Hugh told you about blue balls?

LINDY *(Shyly)*: Sounds crude, I know. But I prefer to know these things. If he's in the mood and I'm not, it's easy enough to just—assist him.

ADAM: May I ask you a question?

LINDY *(Playfully arch)*: I think we've reached a point in the evening where questions can be entertained, yes.

ADAM: I assume you went to college?

LINDY *(Puzzled)*: SMU.

ADAM: And you read books, magazines, keep up with current events?

LINDY: Why?

(She fumbles with ice in the bucket.)

ADAM: Have you ever actually *heard* of a man swelling with pain "down there" because a woman refused to go all the way?

LINDY *(Plopping ice in both glasses, trying to be light)*: Now that you mention it . . .

ADAM *(Half indignant)*: Blue balls! That's from the dark ages of drive-in movies and bee-hive hairdos, guys used it to guilt-trip their dates into bed. You mean your husband, in all seriousness, told you—

LINDY *(Terse)*: Yes, as I said, I am in certain respects, a little naive . . .

ADAM: A little?

LINDY: I wasn't brought up to question things like that, Adam. I was taught to cultivate a look of fascination when a man spoke, but not listen too carefully. You met me at the tippy end of a thirty-year slumber, speaking of Sleeping Beauty.

ADAM: You're the most baffling woman I ever met.

LINDY *(Growing increasingly rankled)*: Okay you made your point: I'm naive; you're worldly. I'm sorry I couldn't go through with it, that's me in my provincial place— moving right along!

ADAM *(Startled by her tone)*: Calm down.

LINDY *(Sharply)*: Never tell me to calm down! Never say that to me, ever!

(She stops, amazed by her outburst.)

(Calmer now) I'm really sorry. On the bed before / it frightened me.

ADAM: Why?

LINDY: For a moment I couldn't remember my life.

ADAM: Isn't that supposed to happen, for a moment?

LINDY: Not like— *(Trying to pin it down)* I was *back then*, in your office; *literally*, us on the futon. I was *there*, Adam, do you understand what I'm saying—like a needle you put back on a record just where you left off, but *years* later. Nothing that happened since then seemed real. I couldn't remember where I *am*. My life. Except vaguely—I'm married, I have children, I live somewhere not-New-York. Part of my brain just fell away. I panicked. I'm okay now. It was a déjà thing. Vu. Déjà voodoo. The old magic. *(Remembering the water glasses)* —Ice water! *(Brings glasses over)* Cheers.

(They clink glasses and drink. The mood is dangerous and raw.)

ADAM: One more question?

LINDY: Something neutral, I hope.

ADAM: This "fling" of ours—isn't that what you called it . . . pretty casual word for something that makes you panic ten years later . . . even fully clothed.

LINDY: Oh. You want to strut, is that it?

ADAM: Was it a fling? Or more than a fling?

LINDY: Look, I'm fully aware—actually *painfully* aware—of the difference between your experience and mine / of our episode in New York.

ADAM: What difference is *that?*

LINDY: Adam, enough. I didn't put out. Okay. You're angry. You've embarrassed me. We're even.

ADAM: Why *embarrassed?*

LINDY: I think that's pretty obvious: "Married Matron Plans Torrid Night with Ex-Lover"—the simplest encounter on earth this side of *Peyton Place*—dinner sex and *au revoir?* And she can't even pull it off.

ADAM: Yes, I got that, but what's the problem?

LINDY: Too many memories. You bring back that whole year. The craziness, the excitement. All those amazing people—

ADAM: Like yourself?

LINDY: In my dreams.

ADAM: Lindy, you were head and shoulders above half the East Village Pseuds I ran with. You were a published poet, for god sake.

LINDY: Not published—xeroxed, stapled in the corner and sold in three downtown bookstores, run by pasty-looking macrobiotics with too much nostril hair.

ADAM: The *Village Voice* called you Emily Dickinson on angel dust.

LINDY: "Ecstasy," darling. Don't misquote my best and only mention in the annals of forgotten verse.

ADAM *(Half teasing)*: See, you even talk like a poet.

LINDY: I'm showing off for an appreciative audience; the first in years. *(Beat)* You don't have to flatter me, darling, I knew what I was; a small-town debutante who had the very good luck to land a Hugo Metz. I didn't *need* poetry to say what I had to say, and what I had to say was ordinary. All in all, I'm a pretty ordinary woman.

ADAM: Bullshit.

LINDY *(Becoming agitated)*: Tell me, how many ex-mistresses do you have 'round the country? Are nights like this, one of the perks of success?

ADAM *(Irked)*: Don't try and wriggle off the hook for skipping out on me like that. If it was a casual fling, fine, let's hop into bed and screw for "Auld Lang Syne." But if it meant enough for the memory to freak you out after all these years— I'm sorry, that's no casual fling, Lindy.

LINDY: We had an affair. Of course it meant *something*!

ADAM: Beyond the normal?

LINDY: What's "beyond"? Indeed, what's "normal"?

ADAM: Lindy, look at me.

LINDY *(With rising anger)*: Well, my god, all right—what do *you* think? The way I gave myself, I'm not *that* shameless. Maybe other women you've known, but not this girl, not by a very long shot. I thought you were being tactful back then, not mentioning how over the top I acted when we were together—

ADAM: I had no idea.

LINDY: Oh, please! You purred like a cat afterwards. You knew what you did to me. Look at my nose, for god sake, ten years later I'm still blushing at what a brazen whatever I was—groupie.

ADAM: "Groupie"? You?!

LINDY: Well, weren't you—what was the phrase "the hottest, hippest, happening-est architect in TriBeCaStan"? Isn't that how *Mirabella* put it? And he developed a warm spot for, imagine, a young mother from below the Mason-Dixon Line.

ADAM: How can you be so incredibly off-base? First of all, I never *had* another "mistress." Second, "purring"? I was dumbstruck lying with you, wondering how I ever lucked into a woman like—you were the most ravishing, mysterious person I ever / and with a real grown-up life, two toddlers, a husband on Wall Street. And god knows what arrangement with him . . .

LINDY: You know, if I couldn't see your face right now I'd swear you were putting me on.

ADAM: I thought you got bored with me one day and found a new lover. It took me a year to work up the courage to even track down your number.

LINDY: You called?

ADAM: The line was disconnected.

LINDY: This is so bizarre.

ADAM: I waited to hear from you. For a very long time.

LINDY: This *is* Adam Penzius I'm talking to, right? You don't have an evil twin who used to shave his head and wear lapelless jackets? And waited by the elevator after my first Book Circle to whisper in my ear, "Come with me right now."

ADAM: I'd never done something like that before in my life. Or since.

LINDY *(Studies him a moment, then)*: Adam, stop it, stop teasing, I'm embarrassed . . .

ADAM: Think, Lindy, Lindy . . . Do the authentically hip and happening spend alternate Friday nights in Turtle Bay discussing Philip Roth with dentists and shrinks? No, they party and club and Hamptonize with all the other Shiny Now People.

LINDY: You were looking for clients. Networking. You said.

ADAM: I was. Till you came along.

LINDY: Well—thank you for trying to put me at ease. You're very sweet. And tactful. You could have taught your staff a thing or two.

ADAM: *My* staff?

LINDY: I imagine you're too upscale for body rings and tattoos anymore. Is that guy with the green off-center Mohawk still there? And the G.I. Jane with engineer boots and the big silver safety pin through her cheek?

ADAM *(Laughs)*: Danika and Majjid! No, they disappeared one day. With all the office computers.

LINDY: It looked like a high-end drug-rehab center, that office of yours. I expected a few oxford shirts—a turtleneck, maybe. I even dressed for the occasion—Donna-Karan-casual.

ADAM: Wait. When were you in my office? In daylight, I mean?

LINDY *(Shy)*: Once. Just that— *[once]* / Only one time.

ADAM *(Very curious)*: Which time; you never mentioned—

LINDY *(Trapped)*: It was a spur-of-the-moment thing.

ADAM: Oh?

LINDY *(Torn between reticence and confession)*: I had a lunch downtown . . . I thought, if you had a free moment, we might—

ADAM: We might—?

LINDY: You know, go for coffee, a drink. I sat there on the futon. A pretty bizarre experience in daylight. And clothed. Not to mention vertical. Watching your staff at work. So focused and self-assured, even the bizarros.

ADAM: Why didn't you wait for me?

LINDY: I felt, I don't know . . . *exposed.*

ADAM: No one in the office knew about us. They probably took you for a client, a friend—

LINDY: But *I* knew what I was; a confused woman about to leave her husband. Which would mean her children, too, since the Metz Clan would move legal mountains to win custody of the little Bicycle Heirs.

ADAM *(Trying to work it out)*: You dropped by my office—for a coffee—because you were thinking of leaving your husband?

LINDY: Just testing the water, seeing how it felt to be on the brink of giving up everything for New York, for writing—for you. But I felt trivial finally, watching your colleagues, all these driven people with real skills, with training and ambition. All I had, it suddenly struck me, was some vague dream of being a poet. And a naive notion that I could throw myself on the mercy of a man I barely knew.

ADAM: I was in love with you.

(This hits her like an electric shock.)

LINDY *(Trying for calm)*: Surprise, surprise.

ADAM: I thought you had this ultra-sensitive thing with my moods. How could you miss *that?*

LINDY: If you'd given the smallest sign . . .

ADAM: If.

LINDY: If, if, who knows what might have— It's a long time ago.

ADAM: Except while the needle's back on the record—what about now?

LINDY: Now *tonight?*

(Adam takes a moment to get this out:)

ADAM: *Now*, ten years later.

LINDY: I'm lost. What are you asking?

ADAM *(Carefully)*: Could I see you? When I'm out here?

LINDY: After what just happened?

ADAM: It doesn't have to be sex. I'd like to get reacquainted. That doesn't sound right—we never ended it, did we . . .

LINDY: That's why we're here.

ADAM: To *end* it? I see. You planned this as a farewell fuck?

LINDY: I wouldn't put it so elliptically. But, okay. When you called, it occurred to me the problem was, we never ended it. People do, usually, don't they? Have a last time together, *knowing* it's the last time. Doing whatever people do: get sad, cry, feel each other slipping away . . . Isn't that customary? Something about closure.

ADAM: But you don't want to make love. So what does that leave? Say good-bye and no sex? Or spend the rest of the night talking—and the rest of our lives wondering what we missed?

LINDY: I didn't have a Plan B.

ADAM *(Carefully)*: I do. Actually, it was closer to a long-term Plan A.

LINDY *(Smiles, curious)*: Oh?

ADAM *(On the spot)*: Do you have the key to that bar thing?

LINDY: It's open.

ADAM *(Crossing to the mini bar)*: Can I get you something?

LINDY *(Sing-song)*: Plan A?

(Adam finds a miniature scotch bottle in the mini bar.)

ADAM: Do you happen to remember a Friday, after, I think it was, *Madame Bovary?* . . .

LINDY *(Smiling)*: *Bright Lights, Big City.*

ADAM: Yes! *(Then)* You know what I'm talking about?

LINDY: Of course.

ADAM *(Opens the bottle)*: Well?

LINDY *(Mocking)*: Well?!

(He downs the tiny bottle, then opens another.)

ADAM: Were you . . . at all serious? Because *I* was.

LINDY: At the time, yes. In that way lovers are, when they say those things.

ADAM: I wasn't aware we were so statistically average.

LINDY: Isn't that the point of an affair, to make something ordinary feel like the first time ever?

ADAM: It was more than that. We vowed we'd always have each other while the rest of our life went on. It was a marriage, Lindy. A secret marriage.

LINDY: Yes, that was sweet.

ADAM: I've thought a lot about that idea over the years. More and more in fact. What a good thing it might have been—

LINDY: Another fairy tale.

ADAM: No, I've *seen* it. My partner's dad comes to town on business a couple three times a year. And once up in Riverdale, way off the beaten path, inspecting a job site, I saw him go into a restaurant with his arm around this plump, smiley white-haired lady with pink cheeks, you know, wire-rim glasses, one of those jolly-sexy-older-liberal-lady types. Herman turned and saw me. He's married, you see. I know his wife. She's great. They're a total family-family. My partner still thinks growing up with them ruined his chances for marriage because he'll never be as happy with someone as his folks are with each other, and it's true, they're happy. But there's his old dad—oh, right, six months later he treated our office to dinner, he's in town *with his wife* this time, and when I go in the men's room he's right behind me—boom— into the next stall: "The woman you saw me with, we've been lovers for thirty-seven years. No one knows, not even my kid, you got that?" And he walks out. I found him back at the table with his arm around his wife . . . he loves her, too. Herman is an ordinary guy. Husband, provider—solid citizen. It's *not* a fairy tale.

LINDY *(Studying him; then finally)*: No.

ADAM: I want you back.

LINDY: No, Adam.

ADAM: Why not?

LINDY: I can't even handle a casual night.

ADAM: A casual *farewell* night. This is different—

LINDY: Adam, you don't know . . . you can't begin to imagine how on the edge / I was *lost* after New York. Do you understand? Not immediately, not *right* after, but . . . *(Thinks back)* Actually it was just a *sadness* at first, very slight. Which I took to be . . . the lack of a lover. I'd never had one before you, so I didn't know the signs. And I figured, okay, maybe what I need is someone to replace you, and practical-minded Lindy that I am, I found, *chose* actually, with cold-blooded calculation—poor man—the curator of the Plains Indian Museum. I'm on the board, so no eyebrows rose over the odd meeting. And he was discreet, attentive . . . a thoroughly adequate choice, except for his aftershave, which smelled like banana. Not an erotic scent, I discovered. The problem was, there was no urgency about our meeting. Nothing about him felt *necessary*. And this vague sadness inside, it was still there. So I ended it one day. Very cordial, *"Au revoir,* thanks for the sex, see you at the next board meeting." Then out in the parking lot I started towards my car and . . . collapsed. Fell down in the snow, desolate. Thinking of you. Buried under this tidal wave of grief.

(Adam doesn't know how to comfort her.)

And with a family to manage. I had to schedule suffering between dishes and laundry. God save anyone from going through what I had to getting over you—without letting it show. Waking the kids. Making breakfast, packing lunch, getting them off to school in time to drive somewhere alone and lie down behind the steering wheel, sobbing. Making love to your husband when every inch of you feels numb. Watching him move over you, and collapse, and you feel nothing at all. *(Really facing him now)* I'll never put myself through that again.

ADAM: You won't have to. *(Showing his beeper)* I'm a beeper away. We can talk anytime.

LINDY: No, Adam. Tonight settled one thing. It's all or nothing with us. And since it can't be all . . .

(Adam rises, walks around agitated, lost.)

ADAM: How the hell did we get here so fast? I had this whole thing worked out to happen over months, we'd get to know each other, and if all went well, okay, maybe we'd . . . reconnect fully after half a year at least, certainly that long before a night like— You're right, we *do* snowball.

LINDY *(Holding her glass)*: Speaking of which, my ice is melted.

ADAM: Lindy, we should say good night.

LINDY *(A little too fast)*: Now?

ADAM: Let's give ourselves breathing room, time to cool off. Now that we know what happens with us, still—we could have a good night's sleep, let all this sink in. Decide how we feel about—seeing more of each other. And how much more. Then . . . I'll call you in the morning and see if you'd still like to have breakfast with me. How does that sound?

LINDY *(Disappointed)*: Deeply responsible.

ADAM: And then, if the morning goes well / a step at a time.

LINDY: Let's not plan beyond breakfast.

ADAM: Breakfast. Sure.

LINDY: Eight-ish?

ADAM *(Stalling)*: Don't you want to sleep late? Sunday?

LINDY: Trained by kids. Six-thirty, boi-oy-oy-oing, eyes open, hit the ground running.

ADAM *(He smiles)*: I'll jog, I'll shower, then I'll call. *(Beat)* Eight-fifteen.

LINDY *(Wryly)*: You jog?

ADAM: At my age it takes work to keep in shape.

LINDY: And whom for in-this-shape do we keep?

ADAM: You're wicked, Lindy. Thanks for—for dinner.

LINDY: My pleasure. *(Thinks)* Entirely, I'm afraid. *(Opens the door, peering out into the hall)* All clear.

ADAM: Would you mind—a quick good night kiss.

LINDY: A quick one.

(They kiss lightly, but too long, her hands opening at her side.)

ADAM: Good night, Lindy.

LINDY: Good night, Adam.

(Adam moves to the door, opens it to leave, but turns back and looks at her. The lights dim.)

SCENE 3

Later.

Lindy and Adam lie entangled in bed, covers bunched and gathered around them concealing much, but not all of their naked bodies.

The food trolley remains, their half-eaten meal as we last saw it. Clothes lie everywhere.

Silence. Breathing. Stilless. Then:

LINDY: I have bad news.
ADAM: No!
LINDY: My leg.
ADAM: Don't say it.
LINDY: Asleep. Sorry.
ADAM: All right, all right. Fast or slow?
LINDY: Medium.
ADAM: On a count of three?
LINDY AND ADAM: One . . . two . . . *three*!

(Lindy pulls back her hips with a shudder of pleasure-pain.)

LINDY: I *hate* this part.

(She sits up, kneading her leg.)

ADAM: *You* hate it!? I'm the one out here in the cold, all shriveled and sad.

LINDY *(Peeking under the covers)*: They're such funny little things. Like a furry animal with a life all its own.

ADAM *(Pressing down the blanket)*: The image isn't helpful right now.

LINDY: I wonder what it would be like to have one of my own?

ADAM: You'd be a morphadyke.

LINDY: "Morphadyke"?

ADAM: Roo's word. They did earthworms in science. He couldn't believe two sexes in the same body.

LINDY: Ahhh, "morphadyke." Nice.

ADAM: I asked if he knew what made men and women different. "Males go out and you see everything, females go in so you have to guess." That's what he said.

LINDY: I like this boy.

ADAM: Me, too. A lot.

(Lindy rises, wrapping a sheet around her.)

Why the sheet?

LINDY: At our age, modesty is advised. Out of bed, anyway.

(She stands and takes a step, wobbling.)

ADAM: Still asleep?

LINDY: That ain't sleep, darlin', it's Wobbly Knees, the Push-Button Cow. Feeling extremely, "Moo."

(She chuckles while hobbling around to get circulation back in her legs.)

How did we manage this every other Friday? Where did we find the energy?

(She sits at the table, smiling, basking.)

ADAM: We rise to the occasion.
LINDY: Bliss. Utter . . . complete . . . obscene . . . perfect bliss. I bet we're the only guests awake right now. Maybe in the whole state. What if we were the last people on earth? Would that be nice, would you like that, Adam?

(Adam is silent.)

Adam?!
ADAM *(Startled awake)*: Hello?
LINDY: Don't you dare fall asleep on me.
ADAM *(Dreamily)*: I was checking my eyelids for holes.
LINDY *(Idly picking food from plates, nibbling)*: All you men want to do is doze off afterwards. Honestly!
ADAM: And what do "you *women*" want to do . . . *afterwards*?
LINDY: Talk, dance, fight a war!
ADAM: You'd win, no contest. Just get all the women in the world to put out for all the guys at once and when they fall asleep afterwards, kill 'em.

(Lindy starts cutting her steak.)

LINDY: I wrote some poems about us.

(Adam takes a moment to hear this, then props himself up. She speaks his imaginary reaction:)

"Oh god, she's going to read to me. I have to listen and pretend it's good. Is this the price of sex?!'" Don't worry, I didn't bring little *Jock and Julienne* with me; that's the title. Isn't it *awful*! Nursery rhymes, kind of, about this little boy and girl lost in a fairy-tale city. Very erotic.

ADAM: I'd like to read them.

LINDY: No.

ADAM: One day?

LINDY: I want you to know they exist is all. That you were in my thoughts. A lot. Next topic.

(She doesn't look at him, resumes slicing meat with renewed concentration.)

ADAM: You seem to be controlling this situation.

LINDY *(Smiling)*: That's 'cause I have a knife.

ADAM: What are you doing over there, Lindy Metz?

LINDY: Cutting red meat into bite-sized chunks. Energy for the night ahead.

ADAM *(Mock horror)*: More!? She wants *more*!?

LINDY: I'm stocking up. Winters out here can be long and cold.

ADAM: We have all tomorrow. And . . . after. Don't we?

(He sits now, looks at her. Beat. Finally:)

LINDY: *And* we have tonight!

(She carries the plate to the bed, sits cross-legged, then places a piece of steak in her mouth, licking her fingers.)

Mmmmmm.

(She takes another slice of meat and holds it out. She feeds him.)

ADAM: You know how I want to spend tomorrow? Actually, it's today already . . . later today? I want to go swimming. The hotel guide mentioned granite quarries a few miles out of town . . .

LINDY: You don't want to see me in a bathing suit, you really don't.

ADAM: Haven't I seen everything already?

LINDY *(With a brief odd look)*: Not by a very long shot.

ADAM: Well at least you're embarrassed. Which means you're thinking about it. That was a trick question to see if you were serious about tomorrow.

(She eats more steak, then feeds him . . .)

Thank you.

LINDY: I like feeding you; you put something in me, I put something in you. "Oh, Mom, you are sooo deep," that's what Doug says when I spin off into one of my little brain-travel things—

(Adam averts his face suddenly. He pulls on his boxer shorts.)

What's the matter? Adam?

(He turns his back to her.)

Is it something I said?

ADAM: No. Give me a second. *(Controlling deep emotion)* I'm not used to being fussed over— / Sorry.

LINDY: A little steak goes a long way with you. I'll have to remember that.

ADAM *(Ignoring her attempt to lighten things)*: Even the smallest things you do, the Goofy Gifts—

LINDY: Any excuse to shop, darlin'.

ADAM: Do you do that for Hugh? Study him, figure out what he'd like?

LINDY (*Again, trying to lighten things*): More steak?

(*She feeds him another piece.*)

ADAM: Amazing. Melinda Metz. There were times I thought I might have made you up. Sometimes at work designing a room I picture the two of us in it wandering around, having dinner, making love. My staff thinks I'm having creative brainstorms. I'm with you, that's all. Even in the morning while I jog, I imagine you running alongside—

LINDY: *Jogging?!* Me?!! Please, adultery's one thing but I draw the line at exercise.

ADAM (*Playing along*): All right, you sleep late, I'll bring home a coffee from Starbucks after my run.

LINDY: That's better, darling. Keep it light and sweet, like my coffee, three sugars. And a chocolate éclair—wouldn't you *die* for a chocolate éclair right now, or one of those strawberries dipped in chocolate, chocolate *anything*, was there any chocolate in the bar?

(*She crosses the room and searches the mini bar.*)

ADAM (*Resuming his previous thought*): In the evening, putting Roo to bed, I imagine you across the room watching me from beside the hamster cage while I horse around tucking him in. A sort of secret friend who sees me being a good father—

LINDY (*Looking in the mini bar*): God, look at all these ways to get fat.

ADAM: Family's all I ever really wanted. Success always seemed easy, but to make a family. And hold it together. I'm embarrassed how much I love being in my house, just . . . being there, with my kid, everything snug and safe. I'd picture someone in my life to share that with.

LINDY: Macadamia nuts?—

ADAM: Anyway, the thought of you got me through some pretty bleak nights, and I promised myself, if I ever saw you again, and found the right moment, I'd thank you.

LINDY (*Discovers*): M&Ms!

ADAM: One more thing—

LINDY: I get the point, Adam. You're welcome for whatever I helped you get through.

ADAM: There's so many things we never said in the New York days.

LINDY: Couldn't we just be quiet and eat chocolate together?

ADAM: Are feelings still a forbidden topic?

LINDY: I don't want the past dragged into . . . *right now.* Or the future. Just let's be—quiet. Okay? If you knew how much it means to me to feel this serene. To know it's still possible . . .

ADAM (*Not fully understanding her meaning, but sensing her need*): Then promise me we'll spend tomorrow together.

LINDY: "*Tomorrow*"? That's too far away, I can't picture it.

ADAM: Lindy!

LINDY: Shhh. Eat something. Chocolate. Steak. Get your strength back.

ADAM (*Suddenly challenging*): So we can fuck a few more times before you vanish? For good this time?

LINDY: I guess I can kiss this little calm of mine good-bye.

ADAM: That's the plan, isn't it? Rut and revel till dawn then: "Adios, Sunshine"? How do I know you'll be here when I wake up?

LINDY (*Sharp*): How do I know you have a client in town?

ADAM: What?

LINDY: You could have made him up for all I know. You could have made up the whole job out here.

ADAM: You think I'm crazy?

LINDY: How could I think anything, I barely *know* you! And you certainly don't know me! If you want to picture me as some kind of nourishing earth-mother type, lurking in your kid's bedroom watching you play daddy, fine, but don't feel you have to share it with me, because all it does is make me wonder what desperate situation sent you chasing out here in the first place— *(Agitated now, and annoyed)* Why did you have to start?! It was perfect a moment ago!

ADAM: It was perfect ten years ago.

LINDY: It was exactly *not* perfect or we'd have been able to say the simple things to each other like: "I love you. Be with me. Let's find a way." All we did was hide behind feverish talk about books, then fuck and fuck and fuck for hours on end!

(She stops herself, forcing calm to return.)

ADAM: Let's not make the same mistake again.

LINDY: Oh for pity's sake, Adam, what's wrong, just spit it out? Did you leave your wife? Are you *thinking* of leaving her? Did you just learn you have a fatal illness and I'm your last hurrah?

(They exchange a look, then explode with laughter.)

ADAM: I'm in perfect health. And my marriage is—completely functional.

LINDY: Then what's this all about?

ADAM: I told you—

LINDY: No, no, Adam, you're here because of *me*, right? This job is because of me.

ADAM: Yes and no.

LINDY: Mainly yes.

ADAM: I've known where you were for a few years. I spend a lot of time online these days with Jan on the road. I started searching the web for old schoolmates, girlfriends—one day, there you were. I didn't dare call . . . then this job happened.

LINDY: You see how this puts a certain *pressure* on me? I do have a life, you know.

ADAM: We both do.

LINDY: I don't want this.

ADAM: I don't believe you.

LINDY: You know so little about me.

ADAM: I know you came to my office one day to change your life. I know you made yourself free tomorrow in case seeing me again stirred things. —Okay, it's scary for both of us, so we made up excuses for tonight: "I'm here for a job." Not only a good reason to come, but if the you-and-me part of the trip doesn't work out, I still come home with a job. But *your* ploy, much more cunning: a farewell night. There I'll be lying next to you afterwards with your scent on me, the warmth of your skin, your breath in my ear, knowing I'll lose it all for good if I don't make a move, show my hand. And once you've seen it you can play your cards . . . if you decide to. Am I warm? Hot?

(Without preplanning his tirade, he has blundered his way to the truth.)

LINDY *(Beat)*: Scalding.

ADAM: You're a coward.

LINDY: Just cautious. I think ahead. What if the night with you had turned out—

ADAM: Awful?

LINDY: The opposite. If it turned out like this.

(At last, the full terror and respect their attraction warrants: they kiss and quickly entangle, desire flaring like a struck

match. They stagger toward the bed. She forces herself to stop, now on edge.)

Aren't we too old?

ADAM: *Way* too old.

LINDY: How do we even go about it? I've forgotten the rules!

ADAM: To hell with rules.

LINDY: Oh, Adam, rules are everything: what, when, where, how often?

ADAM: We didn't need them in New York.

LINDY: You're so wrong. From the minute we saw each other at—Dr. Gasarch's?

ADAM: Hecht. The dermatologist. That's where we met.

LINDY *(Animated)*: *Crime and Punishment*, I remember. I never had it come to me so distinctly that I was going to sleep with a man. After that, the whole discussion was about us, about the transgression ahead, the idea of it: *Crime and Punishment.* God what a sexy night.

ADAM *(Remembering)*: Yeah.

LINDY: Then the rules began: "Avoid his eyes." "Cover your tracks." "Don't look at him." "Leave separately." "Disagree with him about the odd book; he says *Gravity's Rainbow* is groundbreaking, argue that it's incomprehensible."

ADAM: You want to know the truth? I never read it.

LINDY: No one *read* the books, Adam. Except you and me. The others came for the food. And I came to show off— to flirt. To make love.

ADAM *(Then)*: Fine; we'll make rules.

LINDY: Are you a good liar?

ADAM *(Not expecting this)*: What kind of question is that?

LINDY: We're putting our families in each other's hands. Can you lie for all of us? 'Cause if we get careless, or desperate, and spill our heart to the person nearest at hand— remember *Crime and Punishment*—the guilty need to confess more than they fear punishment. That's Fyodor, hon, not Melinda. There's three young lives that could get run over by a truck if our little deception gets away from us.

ADAM: You can trust me.

LINDY (*Strangely energized, beyond mischievous*): What'll you tell Jan when you travel?

(*She watches Adam like a scientist studying an animal.*)

ADAM: "I'm away on business."

LINDY (*As Adam's wife*): "To see *that woman*?" (*Herself*) I'm being your wife. She'll figure out what's going on sooner or later, and she'll wait until you're off-guard, then ambush you from behind the coffee pot. (*Relentless, but irresistible*) How do you answer her?

ADAM: She'll never notice.

LINDY: She's human, Adam, she's a woman.

ADAM: She's busy with other things.

LINDY: You mean work? Don't let that fool you. We live from a place that feels everything, even if the eyes don't admit what they see, the heart always knows, and that's where we act from and register every tremor, every inflection. It's the language of people who share a life, even if they never talk—*especially* then—because silence is the ultimate warfare. (*With growing animation*) Can you stand up to complete isolation, darling, the way only a woman hurting badly knows how to isolate, with smiles and touches and little pleasantries, with no feeling behind them except rage? Can you keep your nerve through that? Few men could.

ADAM: What happened to that serene mood you were in?

(*She starts popping M&Ms into her mouth rapidly.*)

LINDY (*Speaking while she chews*): Maybe you're already at war and don't even know it. If she smells that you were never hers to begin with, anything's possible—her career could be revenge on you for waiting ten years to propose. A woman can forgive almost anything except hesitation in desiring her and, my god, after making her wait that long you may have reached a point where the only decent thing left to do was walk away.

(Her animation unnerves him.)

ADAM *(Feeling raw and destabilized)*: I did.

LINDY: You did *what?*

ADAM: I left Jan.

LINDY: No, Adam. Please don't say you're here because—

ADAM *(Growing agitated)*: Not *tonight*, for god sake. *Before.* In New York. I mean, I packed . . . stored a suitcase in a closet at the office. I wrote long notes to myself about how I'd ask you to live with me. Leave your husband, write full-time—my mind was back-and-forth for weeks, one minute thinking you'd laugh at me for being some downtown freak who totally missed the signals, and the next minute I'd think, no, she's unhappy, never talks about her life, if I take her off-guard with a dramatic gesture . . . So I decided finally to risk it.

LINDY: And you got cold feet. Oh-blah-dee.

ADAM: I planned it for the next Book Circle. You weren't there. You missed the next one, too. And the one after.

LINDY: Wait a minute; you don't mean . . . ?

ADAM: You'd left New York.

LINDY: Oh, Adam, that's just the saddest thing I ever heard. *(She sits)* One Friday later and we might have—

ADAM: Who knows. Maybe I'd have got cold feet.

LINDY: Did you really mean to / you're not just saying it to make me feel less like an idiot for . . . having had ideas?

ADAM: I went home that night. Jan was standing at the stove naked, drenched in sweat, eleven-thirty P.M., cooking chili. So out of character. I thought, "Who is this stranger I've been living with for ten years?" The way she watched me come through the door, the fury in her eyes—not *just* fury; need, desperation. It just came out of me, this thing I'd never said, never been able to say before: "I love you."

(Lindy is still, M&Ms in her lap.)

LINDY: In ten years you never . . . ?

ADAM: Neither of us. We didn't—*say* those things. But that night something changed for a moment. We were naked, in a trance—no, it was more like a physical *place*— *(Thinks)* Paradise, really.

LINDY: Another fairy tale.

ADAM: She got pregnant that night. We didn't know when she left in the morning—dance tour in Yugoslavia. She never called. Never wrote. Not once in two months. And she came back guarded, distant—

LINDY: Why?

ADAM *(With effort)*: Time was running out. You see, she didn't want children. Never had. Two months gone, a choice had to be made—

LINDY *(Understanding)*: Oh, dear—

ADAM: And I won. I watched her lie on her back in bed for three months for something she didn't even want, a terrible, terrible pregnancy. She basically threw away her career for me—

LINDY: Her choice—

ADAM: But *for me*, she did it because *I* wanted a child, because I thought, I told myself, she'll change with motherhood, soften, relax inside. As if a child might make her more the kind of woman she was that one night . . . and I'd love her again.

LINDY: Was it good as us?

ADAM: Ridiculous, right? To think a trip here could solve anything. I'm in the wrong life.

LINDY: Then leave.

ADAM: Not possible.

LINDY: You already did once—almost.

ADAM: Before certain vows were made.

LINDY: Marriage vows are negotiable.

ADAM: To Roo. To my son. He asked me to swear on his life I'd never leave his mom. His best friend's parents just split, he feels the chill in our house. I promised him.

(He watches her, confused suddenly.)

LINDY: Oh, Adam, you didn't!

ADAM *(Feeling totally exposed)*: Talking to you feels more like betrayal than making love, why is that?

LINDY: Words are personal. Sex is just—bodies.

ADAM *(Resolute, precise)*: Here's what I've decided; I need intimacy. I can't find it with my wife. So either I forget that need, or I find a woman I can be close to. And I've decided on the latter.

LINDY *(Laughing)*: Am I a finalist, or was this the first cut?

ADAM: That didn't come out right. What I mean is, don't feel pressured. I want it to be you, but—if you're worried I'm not a good enough liar . . .

LINDY: Poor darling, I was mouthing off, you're not supposed to listen when I get like that.

ADAM: I'm sorry to dump all this on you.

LINDY *(Quieter)*: It's just . . . bad timing.

ADAM: I meant to slip this idea in gradually.

LINDY: I'm flattered by your loss of control. But Hugo needs me right now. Badly. He ran the business into the ground. We're bankrupt.

ADAM: Jesus.

LINDY: We'll hardly end up in the poor house, darling. But he'll need my undivided attention during his run for Congress. Thank god for politics to fall back on when all else fails. Stop, Lindy. That's so damned unfair. I am, though: unfair, demanding, temperamental. He deserved someone lower-maintenance.

ADAM: What a mess.

LINDY: Poor Hugo, so patient and forgiving—so unbearably fucking forgiving. Why should I need forgiveness? I don't forgive *him* for failing. *(Stops)* Oh, dear, I said it. He's a failure. My husband is a failure. He failed in New York, he failed out here. I'm sorry, Adam, but you see what a bitch you lust after?

(She wanders in circles, wiping off objects, trying to tidy her surroundings.)

ADAM: You're upset, who wouldn't be—

LINDY: Don't be insightful and sympathetic; we're *talking* now. God I envy your wife. She married a success. She's the choice of a man who *succeeds*! Whereas I, who chose security, I end up the door prize of a great big zero with pedigree. You know what I actually had in mind tonight, if you showed up here all middle-aged and puffy, I thought I might put the moves on you while I still have allure—which I do, I'm well aware, god knows I work hard enough at it—

ADAM: You were planning to seduce me from Jan?

LINDY: I am that small.

ADAM: Go for it.

LINDY *(Suddenly quiet)*: Not in the cards, darlin'. The most we can hope for is nights like this.

ADAM: Nights? That's plural. Are more nights in store? Is it official, we're having an affair?

(She gazes at him, mesmerized. A faint twerbling noise: the cell phone in her purse. She doesn't respond.)

Lindy?

LINDY *(Abstract)*: Do you hear something?

ADAM: Your phone.

LINDY *(Coming to)*: But I held my calls— *(Thinks, realizes)* Cell phone! Keeshon! Oh lord, I have to take this . . . *(Distracted, as if she's forgotten where phones are kept)*

ADAM: In your handbag.

LINDY: How do I sound, is my voice normal? *(Examines her face closely, squinting in the mirror)* My pupils get huge sometimes, that's another sign, how big are they, I can't see them?

ADAM: Lindy, what's going on?

LINDY *(Chants encouragement to herself, only half aware of Adam)*: I need to be strong for him, we live up to each other, that's our deal.

(Takes the phone out, answers) Hello? *(Looks quickly at Adam)* Oh. —Hi. —No, Hugh, I was asleep. *(Fake yawn)* —Yes, I know my phone was off— What is this, the third degree? —Why this checking up on me at three in the morning? —You can't what? —Oh, poor poopie.

(She talks with increasing speed and animation, soaring with her own words.)

Wait, hold that thought: "I can't sleep because you're not with me and I miss you." That's so sweet, darling, but the thing is, when I *am* home you can't sleep either, but we've somehow shifted the blame for this insomnia to your anxiety about the kids having nightmares, meaning of course "nightmares about the unstable element in their lives—Mom!" And all this emotional drain leaves him too exhausted to focus on his business affairs, do

I have that about right? *(Having become wittily pedantic, the absolute life of the party)* So my question to you would have to be: "With Mrs. Cross-to-Bear out of the picture, shouldn't you sleep *better*, not worse?" Or is this one of those oh so familiar damned-if-I-do-damned-if-I-don't scenarios, whereby I'm a millstone 'round your neck no matter what the fuck I do at home or away, darling— *(She stops, listens)* . . . Hugh?

(She looks worried.)

(Screams) Hugh?!

(She hangs up. Adam watches her.)

Was that a little zig-zaggy? I can get zig-zaggy.

ADAM: You better tell me what's happening, Lindy.

LINDY: I knew the calm was too good to last. There was a time I could fly level for months at a time without chemicals.

(Roots in her handbag, speaking faster:)

This launch feels pretty smooth, relative to some I could name, like the infamous lawn party—when we moved out here to Hugoland. Before his family met me—well, refused to in fact, 'cause Hugh hadn't first run his bride past the Metz Genetic Quality Control Committee. I wanted to rub their noses in chic—Mama Metz and all her lumbering Country Club Tutons: my legendary Black-and-White Party—oh, Adam, you should have seen it: dance band, tent, even the food—pasta with white sauce and black truffles—god it was swank. Not even a freak thunderstorm could blunt the high spirits. It flattened the entire tent, and everyone went racing into the conservatory, but Unflappable Lindy strode forth chin high into the storm and proceeded to re-raise the tent. What could they do but follow me laughing into the downpour, tra-la. Only, when I looked up from wrestling a tent pole, there they were, motionless silhouettes behind the conservatory windows watching me outside in the rain, raving. Tra-la!

(She stops, takes some pills from her handbag.)

ADAM: Jesus!

LINDY: What a way for poor Hugh to learn his vivacious-if-sometimes-moody young bride and mother of the bicycle babies was "chemically challenged." *(Off his look)* Manic-depressive. In the bipolar sense. *(Beat)* He's been very good about it. Considering I never told him. *(Beat)* He wouldn't have married me, you see. *(Jiggling the pill bottle)* Water?

(Adam gets a glass and hands it to her.)

ADAM: It's warm. *(Regarding the pills)* What are those?

LINDY: "Squeezies," I call them. We have pet names for the meds, all us ladies of the Bipolaroid Society, our support group: "zonkers," "hammers." Whatever sends you back to the DGN, the old Dull Gray Nothing—sort of like TV with the sound off. Life without the awful peaks and valleys. Alas, no orgasm, either. Which is why, for gala moments—for *you*—heigh-ho, heigh-ho, it's off the pills we go. And the cow flies over the moon, straight into orbit sometimes. Sorry you had to see this.

(She pops pills and drinks some water.)

They'll kick in by tomorrow. Just taking them helps—psychologically.

(She smiles.)

ADAM: Better?

LINDY: Shall we move on to what you'll find listed in your program as the second-thoughts portion of tonight's entertainment.

ADAM: Second thoughts? *(Smirks)* Oh. Was this supposed to scare me away?

LINDY: It damn well should.

ADAM: Hence the one-night stand? So I'd never learn the horrible truth?

LINDY: Oh, Adam, that was nothing. When I truly launch ... I've been known to staple the curtains and nail the front door shut and crawl under the rug shrieking like a banshee.

ADAM: What if I told you I didn't care.

LINDY: I'd say you were taking gallantry to surreal extremes.

ADAM: Gallantry has nothing to do with it.

LINDY: Are you *kinky*, Adam?

ADAM: Why should I care one way or another? I don't have to bring the bad stuff home with me, it's not my problem, is it?

LINDY *(Beat)*: That would be, what, extreme tact disguised as callous indifference?

ADAM: We'll only have the best of each other. No dirty laundry.

LINDY: I'd wear you down, lover. When I met my husband, he never drank. Steady as an ocean liner, one-speed Hugo. Now—

ADAM *(Approaching her tenderly)*: Come here.

LINDY *(Vulnerable)*: How can I talk you out of this?

(Adam embraces her.)

ADAM: Too late.

LINDY: Lie with me. Hold me for the time we have left.

(As Adam leads her to the bed, the alarm-radio snaps on at top volume, shattering the silence. Lindy leaps up. Adam fumbles with the unit. Lindy acts shocked, electrified. She bumps to the music, with increasing wildness.)

LET IT PLAY!!!

(She dances over to the alarm-radio and turns the volume back up.)

ADAM: Lindy, other guests!!! . . .
LINDY: Who cares!? I paid for this fucking room. Is there a law against partying when you're in the mood, and oh am I ever in the mood for once in god knows how many centuries . . .

(Adam turns off the music.)

Dance with me, sugar!

(She starts back toward the alarm-radio to turn it up. Adam blocks her.)

You're afraid, aren't you. That's better, you're getting smart now.
ADAM: You want everyone to know you had a visitor?!
LINDY: "It was bad enough when I thought I'd have to listen to *poetry* for god sake, now the dizzy bitch wants to *party*!"

(She turns the volume up full.)

Dance, baby, we only have an hour till he gets here.
ADAM: *Who?*

LINDY: My dear husband. He's coming to save Miss-Naughty-Wife. Didn't you hear my tell-tale loony-tune voice on the phone? He did. *(Talking louder and louder)* He hears every ping in the drive chain. He even knows when I've skipped my meds so I can feel alive for a change—

(She dances over to the table and gets steak from her plate and feeds him.)

Open wide, baby-baby. Let me feed you. Let me sit in a corner and watch you play "Daddy-Waddy-Kins." Come on, lover, eat my meat, get strong and warm and safe with me, Adam, please please god, let someone in the world feel safe with me!

(She forces him to eat. Her strength is unnatural.)

ADAM: Lindy . . . I can't breathe.

(He throws her back. Lindy is stunned.)

LINDY: Oh, shit— *(Shaking violently)* Grab me, hold my arms tight against my body.
ADAM *(Embracing her from behind)*: I'm here.
LINDY: Get me in the shower, as hot as you can make it.
ADAM *(Helping her)*: No problem, tell me what you need . . .
LINDY *(At her wit's end)*: There's so little of me missing. You can barely see it under a microscope. It's so fucking unfair. Don't leave me alone . . .
ADAM *(Steering her to the bathroom)*: I'm here, Lindy. I won't go away. I'm right here. Right here.

(They're in the bathroom. The lights dim.)

SCENE 4

Later.

Lindy dozes in bed, propped on pillows, hair wet. Adam sits vigil on a nearby chair, his hair also wet. Both wear fluffy white terrycloth robes with hotel coat of arms.

Lindy's eyes blink open. She sees Adam watching her.

LINDY *(Groggy)*: Hi.

ADAM: Better?

LINDY: How bad was it?

(He waves the question away.)

ADAM: What can I get you? Water? Cold coffee?

LINDY: You're good at this. It's not gone unnoticed.

ADAM *(Checking his watch)*: Is it too early to order breakfast? I'm starving.

LINDY *(Suddenly alert)*: Oh christ, Adam, you shouldn't be
here, not now.

(She notes the time, relaxes a little.)

Fifteen minutes? I thought I slept—it felt like hours.

ADAM: I get the whole morning with you, you promised.

LINDY: Put your clothes on. We have to clean up the evidence
(Mind racing) —The Interstate at this hour—on Sunday! He could be here any minute.

ADAM: Who?

LINDY: My husband, I *told* you . . .

ADAM: I thought that was just part of the—

LINDY: Did he call back while I was asleep? If he's not sure
I launched, he could phone back and double check before
he saddles the pony.

ADAM: No calls.

LINDY: Then he's on his way. *(Realizing!)* No calls??!! *(Eureka!)*
Keeshon got through the night. Bravo.

ADAM: What'll you do when he arrives?

*(She lifts the cover off and swings her legs heavily over the
side of the bed.)*

LINDY: Don't worry, I'm an old hand at handling Der Hugo.

(She rises and gets her balance.)

Did I say anything unforgivable? I'm told I can get pretty
brutal in full vent.

ADAM: I only remember the good parts.

LINDY: You're so full of it, Adam. Bless you.

ADAM: Are you more or less / back to—?

LINDY: Normal, yes; *my* normal. You'd better get dressed.

(She puts dishes on the trolley. Adam starts dressing. An uneasy silence.)

ADAM: About these rules of ours. Am I allowed to call your office? How much lead time do you need before I come out?

(Lindy loads dishes, her mood remote.)

LINDY *(Finally)*: Let's not make this harder than it is.
ADAM: I'll be back in a few weeks. Three at the outside. I'll leave you my beeper number.
LINDY *(A smile)*: Your *beeper*! Aren't we getting personal!
ADAM: So you can reach me if, in case, you know—
LINDY: I'm teasing. By all means, leave me your beeper.

(Adam stops dressing, alert to her tone.)

ADAM: So . . . it's settled? We're lovers.
LINDY: Say good-bye, Adam.
ADAM: You can't change your mind again. I won't let you.
LINDY: Is that a threat? What'll you do, call my home and breathe into the answering machine?
ADAM: I could, you know.
LINDY *(Not sure this is a joke)*: I guess we're at each other's mercy now.
ADAM: I love you.
LINDY: But it costs you nothing, Adam. A phone call, a few lies, a plane ticket. For me every visit means two days off medication, plus all that self-monitoring while the pills wear down, watching for signs of lift-off . . .
ADAM: Why would every visit have to be all or nothing? We'll mix it up; some days for carnival, other times just a quiet weekend together—a little TV with the sound off—

(She stops clearing the dishes for a moment and studies him.)

LINDY: I don't need you for Dull Gray. I have Hugh for that.

ADAM: But only that. With us there's a choice. You can be wild as you want: dance, talk, eat chocolate, and at the end of the day, no dirty laundry.

LINDY *(Chuckling)*: You are so *male*.

ADAM: I meant to speak for both of us.

LINDY: That's what a fantasy *is*, Adam, when you speak for all the people in it. When they start talking back it's called reality.

ADAM: Isn't this what you want?

LINDY: How long could it last, this place without dirty laundry? Think, darling. What if it keeps being wonderful? How long before the occasional weekend isn't enough and we start wondering why we can't spend a little more time together, then a little more, until finally we'd make something happen, not deliberately, just the way people do, a slip-up, evidence left lying around—

(She sees a tie half under the bed and pulls it out—voilà!)

Or we'd get carried away and lose track of time— *(Noting the time)* Jesus, Adam, get dressed!

(Adam starts to button his shirt, but grows frustrated.)

ADAM: So that's how you talk yourself out of it.

LINDY: What?

ADAM: Everything you want—

LINDY: Careful, Adam—

ADAM: You stack up the problems till there's no way but out, and it feels so wise and prudent that you made the noble sacrifice and saved everyone from a terrible mess. God, what self-deluding crap. People go a whole life looking for what we have, and you're about to throw it away, like you threw poetry away, and New York, and me once upon a time—because you're afraid to take a chance—

LINDY: I'm not afraid.

ADAM: Then what, what the hell is stopping you?

LINDY: I don't think you want to hear this.

ADAM: More surprises, wonderful!!!

LINDY *(Carefully)*: Why did you come here?

ADAM: What part of "I love you" don't you understand? You're everything I want.

LINDY *(Watching him with unnerving intensity)*: For what?

ADAM *(Baffled)*: To be with. To talk to. To love—

LINDY: —honor and cherish? For richer or poorer? *(Smiling, a test)* In sickness and in health?

ADAM: Poetically speaking.

LINDY: In prose, Adam.

ADAM: What are you getting at?

LINDY: This woman you imagine watching you put your kid to bed, making you feel understood—is this your idea of the perfect mistress? 'Cause it sounds to me more like the ideal wife.

ADAM: "Wife"?!

LINDY: You came to kick the tires, darling. To see if I measure up to your dream life, if I'd be someone to leave your marriage for?

ADAM: Whoa, where did "marriage" come from?

LINDY: The same place where you hide everything you don't want to face. You're here to shop for a wife. How scared are you now you've seen the merchandise?

ADAM: I have no intention of leaving Jan.

LINDY: As long as I'm out here to ease the pressure.

ADAM: You're twisting this around.

LINDY: We're not two happy people looking for a now-and-then extramarital squeeze, like your partner's dad and his white-haired bounce. The two of us dream of something very different.

ADAM (*Rallying*): So, your "episode" didn't put me off, time to haul out the "M" word, that's sure to send me running, then whose fault is it that nothing came of tonight?! Is that the game?

LINDY: *You* called *me*, darling.

ADAM: I'm not trying to escape my marriage.

LINDY: Too bad. 'Cause I am. Except I'm not afraid to call it by name. No, that's a lie, I'm terrified. Actually, yes, right now I'm more frightened than I've ever been.

ADAM: Did you plan this from the start?

LINDY: I've only felt complete surrender with one man. I let him get away once. But if I had a second chance—

ADAM: You'd leave Hugh?

(*Lindy comes close, slowly unbuttoning Adam's mis-buttoned shirt, then rebuttoning it correctly, not meeting his eyes, only watching her fingers as she speaks.*)

LINDY: I'm numb from years of taking blame for his failures. My so-called condition's his excuse for everything he can't solve with a smile, a handshake and a high-fiber diet. I've been patient, god knows—while he ran his business into the ground through stubbornness and inattention, claiming I took all his attention, when the simple truth is . . . I'm far stronger than him . . . than most people, in fact. Not much choice: with my chemistry you're either a train wreck, or—remarkable me. And I am, you know, a wonderful wife and mother, for one. My kids are smart and lovely and incredibly tough—not jock tough in the Metz tradition, but deep-inside strong, like their mother. Plus I'm a gifted teacher—my results have been called astonishing. True, I'm a terrible housekeeper. And I tend to put on weight, but I'm a disciplined dieter, plus a great cook, and an awesome hostess. My nose turns red when I'm embarrassed. What else—oh, yes—I'm missing a tiny strand of protein in my DNA which renders me a little wobbly 'round the axis on occasion, but these are tiny flaws.

ADAM: What's going on here, Lindy?

LINDY: I'm buttoning your shirt.

ADAM: No, what are you . . . *saying?*

LINDY: Are you catching my jitters? 'Cause I'm catching your calm.

ADAM: Is this chemicals or something deliberate?

LINDY: I'm listing my qualifications. On the whole I'm an amazing catch, and I'd like to spend what's left of my life with a man who appreciates me, and knows that "different" isn't something to fear, since he went his own way and made a success of being different—

ADAM: I'm not afraid.

LINDY: Then why the affair-for-life? Why the promise to your son? Why all these tricks to keep distance between us. Intimacy takes courage. You can't put furniture in the doorway.

(She pats his shirt and steps back.)

(Admiring her work) There, that's better.

ADAM: Lindy—

LINDY: It's not me who's afraid, Adam. It's you.

ADAM *(Finally becoming worked up, circling her)*: I don't believe this! Back in New York you're too frightened to call and say good-bye, and now after one night together—

LINDY: One night and ten years—

ADAM: Don't get clever. You'd never leave your husband, your kids, just like that—

LINDY *(Rueful)*: If you say so.

ADAM: It's just . . . not like you.

LINDY: One more of the many things you don't know about me.

ADAM: You'd leave your whole life behind and—

LINDY: I'd marry you. I'd make a home for us, yes. And take care of you in the best tradition of a good Cranbrook Deb, every vase with well-chosen flowers. Maybe one day introduce you to my children, and hope they'd learn from a man who'd made something of his life. Maybe even get to know your son in time—all that messy stuff. With luck we'd grow old together. I'd die one minute after you so you'd never be alone, and I'd have no time for a broken heart. You see, you're not the only one with embarrassing fantasies.

ADAM: But would you *do* it. If I said pack your bag right now—

LINDY: Say it. I dare you.

ADAM *(Beat)*: How did we get to this?

LINDY *(Sure he's wriggling out)*: Have you forgotten anything: socks, wallet, credit card?

ADAM: Dry your hair, get dressed, pack. Come with me. Now.

LINDY: Careful, Adam. For a moment I almost believed you.

ADAM: We'll rent a car, drive somewhere, figure out the next step . . .

LINDY: Adam, for god sake, think what you're saying.

ADAM: I've spent my whole life, thinking—thinking and analyzing—weighing the options, and by the time I decide what to do it's either the wrong choice, or I'm too late. I want you, Lindy. It's why I'm here, you're right. I want you.

LINDY: I appreciate the ardor—

ADAM: No more slipaway tricks.

LINDY: I'm talking about practical things—

ADAM: I'm talking about everything else. I wish you were whole and perfect, I wish I hadn't made a mess of my personal life, and I'm scared shitless. I mean this could

be the biggest mistake I'll ever make, but I don't care.
I want you.

LINDY: This is so very dangerous.

ADAM: Tell me anything worth doing that couldn't potentially
fuck up your whole life.

LINDY: All right, Adam. All right.

ADAM: You'll come?

LINDY: Yes. *(Reeling)* I'll get dressed—

ADAM: Throw on a coat, no one'll see at this hour—

LINDY: I can't sneak away like that, naked under a coat?!

ADAM: Why not . . . like old times.

LINDY *(Starting to sink in)*: But it's not, it's not old times, we
can't undo what we do now. We need some time.

ADAM: For what?

LINDY *(Sheds her robe, begins to dress)*: To make arrangements,
explain, you know—everything. I have Hugh, the boys;
you have Greg, it's only fair.

ADAM: No. You'll get scared and bargain away the chance.
I know this game: "It can't be real!" "It won't last."
That's how you ended up with Hugh, and me with Jan,
we never chose, we got scared and settled, and ever since
it's been about—yeah, you're right, rules, but the wrong
rules. Being mature, doing the right thing, knowing our
life doesn't work, but too afraid to put it right because . . .
why? We might upset all the people making us unhappy
to begin with. What if we decide tonight that happiness
has nothing to do with being good; it's about knowing
exactly what we want. We can choose, Lindy, right now,
we can choose, you and me, and leave the rest of our life
for second thoughts.

LINDY *(Beat)*: He'll be here any minute.

ADAM: I don't care. I've been a good man, a good provider, a
good architect—and fuck all of it. Pack your bags.

LINDY: I'll come with you. But not tonight. We have to do
this right.

ADAM: I can't leave you.

LINDY: Trust me, Adam. One week.

ADAM: Five days.

LINDY *(Smiles)*: Five days.

ADAM: Four?

(Their humor returns.)

LINDY: You're insane.

ADAM: Look who's talking.

LINDY *(Beat)*: This'll be headline news in *Bicycle Monthly*.

ADAM: Come here.

(He moves forward to kiss her, but she slips away, needing to make some distance.

She roots in her handbag and finds an envelope. She hands it to him.)

LINDY: My poems.

ADAM: They were here all night.

LINDY: I wasn't sure I wanted you to know so much about me. *(Smiling)* But now the cow's out of the bag.

ADAM: Is this "instead of you."

LINDY: And will you still want me five days from now? All that.

(Adam takes the poems.

Lindy picks up the phone and dials.)

ADAM: Don't bother calling a cab. I'll walk.

LINDY *(On the phone, with authority)*: Desk? —Yes, someone left a food trolley in the hallway, would you kindly remove it. —I know normal room service hours, but it's disgraceful, a hotel of your standing to leave dangerous clutter in the hallway. —May I speak to the night manager? —I agree, there *is* no need for that. —Thank you. *(Hangs up)*

(Turning to Adam, with a smirk) I'm a terror on committees.

(She begins to roll the trolley toward the door.)

ADAM *(Taking the trolley)*: I'll do it. You should get dressed.

LINDY *(Ignoring his offer)*: A *man* wheeling a trolley from the room of Melinda Metz?! What would the neighbors say?

ADAM: Neighbors at three in the morning?

LINDY: Little by little, one comes to realize that all the best people on earth are awake at this hour.

(Lindy wheels the trolley to the door. Adam puts on his shoes. She opens the door, then checks the hallway. She rolls the trolley out.

Adam picks up the cow and idly pushes its button a few times. Lindy returns, supplying a sound effect:)

"Mooo . . . ?"

(She closes the door.)

ADAM *(Lost)*: Lindy—

LINDY: I have a whole other life to get straight in my head and only minutes to do it . . .

ADAM: You'll call?

LINDY *(Distracted)*: He's arriving any second, Adam, you must stay—*go.* I mean *go. (Trembling)* I'm barely holding on.

(Adam, holding her poems, peers out the door.)

ADAM: All clear.

(He opens the door wider. Lindy leans toward him. They kiss lightly. Then more intensely. He breaks free.)

(Urgently) Come with me!
LINDY: Soon. I promise. For god sakes, Adam, go.

(They stand in the open door, staring at each other, held in a motionless thrall.
    The lights dim to black.)

END OF PLAY

FIFTY WORDS

Fifty Words received its world premiere on September 10, 2008, by MCC Theater (Robert LuPone and Bernard Telsey, Artistic Directors; Blake West, Executive Director) at the Lucille Lortel Theatre in New York. It was directed by Austin Pendleton; the scenic design was by Neil Patel, the costume design was by Mimi O'Donnell, the lighting design was by Michelle Habeck, the sound design was by Fitz Patton, the original music was by Josh Schmidt; the production manager was B. D. White, the production stage manager was Pamela Edington. The cast was:

JAN	Elizabeth Marvel
ADAM	Norbert Leo Butz

SCENE 1

A renovated brownstone. The interior design is modern-mixed-with-antique. On one side is the kitchen and preparation island. On the other side is a large dining-room table with artfully chosen mismatched chairs. A stairway behind the table goes to the rest of the house above.

At center is a column with a wall-mounted telephone. Its long cord allows you to walk far in either direction.

A modern clock on a bare wall reads: 9:10 P.M.

Adam prepares something on the island. Janine (Jan) is on the phone, in a light outdoor overcoat, just home.

JAN *(Into the phone)*: I love you, too, cute stuff, very very— yes. / More! *(Beat)* More! *(Beat)* Even more! *(She chuckles)* A million gazillion times infinity. *(Beat. Listening)* What video? *(Listens)* Is that with monsters, I don't want you watching monsters right before bed. *(Listens)* Okay, but if you get scared ask them to turn it off and you read a book or something, okay? And brush your teeth, don't forget. *(Listens)* You just told him good night. *(Smirking)* Okay, one more time.

(She holds out the phone to Adam.)

ADAM *(Calling to the phone)*: 'Night, Roo.
JAN *(Into the phone)*: Big kisses, mwwwah. Mwah-mwah-mwah.

(She hangs up.)

You let him bring his hamster to a sleepover!?

(She removes her coat, folding it neatly over a chair back, and sets up her paperwork and laptop at the end of the table farthest from the island, but facing it, while Adam searches shelves above and below the countertop.)

ADAM: Didn't you get some new bowls, bright-with-covers?
JAN: You carried that humongous cage all the way to Staten Island?
ADAM: I didn't physically carry it from Brooklyn to Staten Island, no; I called a car service and—
JAN: Why would you let him bring a pet to a sleepover, it's such an imposition!
ADAM: You know how he is about that animal.
JAN: It's so unnecessary. You're spoiling him.
ADAM: He thinks Smokey can't sleep unless they're together in the same room. I explained about, you know, the Pelligrinis invited *you*, not you *and a hamster*, maybe someone there's allergic to hamster fur, like Mom is, maybe a sleepover isn't something you bring a house pet to, and then I heard myself talking about sleepover etiquette, as if I knew all about it, like I'd actually ever had a sleepover when I was a kid—Dad, the expert— ridiculous.

(He finds the bowls.)

Ahah, here they are. *(Holds one up to the light)* These are really beautiful. Where'd you find them?

JAN: Why? You wouldn't know if I told you.

ADAM: Probably not. Probably, what I was trying to say is oh, something vaguely complimentary without seeming kiss-ass, since you hate overt flattery, *"Look what good taste my wife has, what a babe, what a—"*

JAN *(Amused)*: I know I have good taste. You don't need to tell me that.

ADAM: My point / I love your taste. You have great taste. I was trying to slip it into the flow of conversation without— Forget it.

JAN: It's such a lame thing to say. I mean thank you, but—

ADAM: You're welcome.

(Adam fusses on the counter. A moment goes by.)

Anyway, as I was / what was I saying, oh right, the Pelligrinis, I called them—about the visiting rodent— and they said, *(Italian accent)* *"Owah, Joey love 'amsters, we 'ave-a tree, 'amsters, they love fennel"*—big warm Italian laugh . . . so much for that problem.

JAN: He's way too attached to that animal—

ADAM *(Emphatic)*: So much. For that. Problem.

(They exchange a quick look—"Shall-we-drop-this?" She gets plates from the cabinet.)

JAN: You have things to do, you have to pack, line up a car to LaGuardia, Greg shouldn't expect you to drop everything and deal with his hamster when you're flying out of town in the morning.

ADAM: He didn't "expect" anything, Jan—

JAN *(Interrupting)*: Why do we need bowls? Just set the cartons on a tray with spoons.

ADAM: I'd like bowls tonight.

JAN: Then you'll have to wash up, because I'm way behind on my lists.

ADAM: I'll take full responsibility for the cleanup.

JAN: Famous last words. Is there any white in the fridge? *[wine]*

ADAM *(Looking)*: Yes.

JAN: Pour me?

(He brings a bottle from the fridge. He watches her.)

(Noticing him) What are you looking at?

(He holds up a champagne bottle and two flutes.)

Champagne? Why?

ADAM: Do I need a reason?

JAN *(Baffled)*: I get nervous when you celebrate randomly.

ADAM: Didn't the What's-It-Group agree to sell you their entire Northeast client list?

JAN: That was three weeks ago.

ADAM: Yeah, but I had to travel then, and you were frazzled and—and Greg wasn't away at his first sleepover.

JAN *(Understanding)*: *I see.*

ADAM: And do you have any particular feelings about what *you see?*

JAN: You're such a goofbag.

ADAM: "Goofbag"? You haven't called me that in years.

(He kisses her and fondles her breast.)

In case there's any ambiguity, that was foreplay.

(He starts to untwist the cork, which pops loudly. Jan yelps; a reflex.)

God I'm good, aren't I?

(He starts to pour.)

JAN: What's gotten into you?

ADAM: My wife. Our life. And Greg has a pal at last, hallelujah. He's out of the house all night for the first time in can-you-believe-it nine-plus years?! One, or several of these things have gotten into me.

(He hands her a full glass to toast with.)

To my incredible wife who, if she's willing, I'll seduce tonight, starting now, going on through dinner and then continuing smoothly upstairs to the bedroom with the exquisite chosen-by-her floral-pattern wallpaper. Cheers.

JAN *(Clicking glasses)*: You should go away more often. No. I take that back. You've been gone too much.

ADAM *(Raising his glass)*: Wherever the work is, and lucky to have it.

(Adam gets the Chinese food while Jan sets plates neatly on the table. She smoothes the tablecloth. The room is suddenly quiet. Jan feels uncomfortable.)

JAN: Did Greg finish his map of Spain?

ADAM: You're asking me?

JAN: You were supposed to check that it was completed and sign it. We promised Mrs. Orfitz he'd finish it tonight—

ADAM: It's Friday. Who does homework Friday night? He has the whole weekend.

JAN: Adam, he's two weeks late.

ADAM: We'll tell Mrs. Orifice he did it tonight. He came running home all, "I have to finish my map of Spain, please don't make me watch TV or go online . . ."

JAN: I don't want another call from school about, "*Is there some problem at home, Greg doesn't seem to be getting his homework done.*"

ADAM: God forbid the school should judge our home and find it wanting.

JAN: What does *that* mean?

ADAM *(Brushing it off)*: Nothing. *(Then)* No, not nothing. Where the fuck do they get off calling Greg's homework performance a sign of problems at home? We shell out enough money to feed a small African nation every year to educate Greg, and every fucking time there's a problem they spin 'round and fire it back at us, "*Greg doesn't seem to understand what he's being assigned in class, we're wondering if there's some problem at home that might explain his sudden psychopathic inattention?*" *(His reply)* "No. There's no problem at home. In fact, there's no problem with Greg, either." A problem would be—let's see, in my school it was Ollie Shultz firing his .22-pistol at kids in the toilet stalls, or Mitchell Drake stabbing kids in the leg with his penknife if they didn't let him lean over them and copy homework; *that* was a problem. And the headmaster's solution was very simple—"*Don't sit next to Mitchell Drake,*" and, "*Use a different bathroom.*"

JAN: Fine, but this isn't some experimental commune school in suburban Portland. That's what you escaped, remember? And what you wanted for Greg was a structured, traditional school environment, which is what we have, and part of the deal with a school like this is meeting their requirements, one of which is homework.

(Adam almost argues back, then controls himself.)

ADAM: Why does this always happen? The night before a
business trip, we start an argument and I leave on a note
of tension.

JAN: What a stupid thing to say. We don't always argue.

ADAM: Tell me one time we didn't have a fight when I was
flying in the morning? I actually use the time packing to
think up ways around it: *If I don't mention work, if I say
something flattering, if I bring dinner home so she doesn't
have to cook*—nothing works.

JAN: If you'd just take Greg's problem seriously.

ADAM: It's his first sleepover. Finally-finally-finally Greg has a
friend. This is a wonderful thing. Let him enjoy it without
worrying about some map of Spain he has to draw for Mrs.
Fucking-Ortho-Face or whatever her name is.

JAN: And when he gets home, who has to tell him, "No computer
till your map's done"? Who has to play bad cop while nice
Daddy is off drawing houses for clients in the Midwest?

ADAM *(Restraining himself)*: Could we just . . . maybe . . .
(Thinks) . . . light some candles?

JAN *(Relenting)*: You know where they are?

ADAM *(Smiling)*: Yes.

*(Adam brings over the meal in bowls and sets it on the
table. Jan brings out candles. They work in silence.)*

Your crazy mom called.

JAN: Oh god—we just talked this morning.

ADAM: She won't stop till you say yes. It's important to her.

JAN: I don't need you to tell me what's important to my
mother, thank you.

ADAM: Something like that would look good on your business
card: "Recipient of the Historical Society Annual Outstanding Achievement for Women in America Award."

JAN: For the most amazing daughter of St. Augustine who did
a tiny bit more than marry and have kids.

ADAM: Don't undervalue yourself, Jan.

JAN: I hate shams. My mother's president of the society, that's why I'm getting the award, she leaned on them, and when Mother leans— Look, I don't want my nose rubbed in my achievements, not when, look at my best friends / Susie's a Supreme Court Justice in Arizona, Solana's chief neurosurgeon in Dallas Memorial, and, *"Oh, Janine Lightner, wasn't she a dancer up in New York for a few years—"*

ADAM: Your mom's very proud of you. *(Smiles)* Very *crazy* and very proud. *(Mimes phone to ear)* "Could you ask my daughter if she could get down here a day early for that award so I can show her the red Datsun convertible I'm very seriously considering for our major spring purchase, well it's not red exactly except I suppose there's all kinds of colors you could call red, this one's more a bright kind of vibrant ripe cherry color you know when cherries are almost *too ripe* more like purple, that's the best time to eat them, at least *I* think so, when they turn the color of those beads on the slippers we bought back from Fez last summer, that was a magical wonderful trip, did I send you the pictures, I had three sets made, Morocco is such an exotic country, maybe not to a New Yorker like you, although of course we have a lot of Spanish influence here in St. Augustine, when are you coming to visit us, Adam, we'd love to see that sweet little Gregory, the electric golf cart's all plugged in and waiting for him . . ." —Shall I go on?

(Jan smiles.)

JAN: She just holds the phone to her brain and lets you listen.

ADAM *(Fondly, quietly)*: I miss you.

(The tone turns intimate.)

JAN: So. The job's going well?

ADAM: Hard to tell. It's the Midwest, so enthusiasm isn't exactly a defining trait of my clients, but the project manager let it drop that I was pretty darn nice for someone from my neck of the woods. Meaning, the East.

JAN: I can't picture you dealing with those people.

ADAM: Why?

JAN: They're just—they're normal folk.

ADAM: And? So?

JAN: You're such a bizarro.

ADAM: What's that supposed to mean?

JAN: I thought you were proud of it.

ADAM *(Beat)*: Okay, now let's just— This is how arguments start, isn't it. Some stupid little putdown, and I take the bait and then / can't we just maybe— What if we change the subject? What if I propose a toast, could I do that, to your amazing success as a startup business.

JAN *(Proud but shy)*: Beginner's luck.

ADAM: No luck about it. I'll wear a wire to school one day when I drop off Greg. You won't believe what the moms say about you, "*Jan is so amazing. How does she do it? Where does she find the energy, the fundraising, the book drive, and she always looks so stylish, even in jeans, what's her secret?*" You're an impressive woman—

JAN *(Embarrassed and pleased)*: Yeah well. Whatever.

ADAM *(Raising his glass)*: To: "Whatever."

(She looks at him with cautious appreciation, but she is also wary.)

JAN: Tim called.

ADAM: Tim? Called here? Why, he never calls here?

JAN: My exact thought.

ADAM: What did he want? Did he say?

(She lights the candles.)

JAN: He wondered if I felt you were overdoing the travel lately.

ADAM: "Overdoing the travel"? He asked you that, he actually / Jesus, what a / there's no name for / he's devious and cheap and, why can't he just— You know two years ago when I finished that museum extension in San Gabriel, guess what he did at the office party? We're toasting this major success and he hands me / I still can't believe it, I'm saying it and I can't believe it / he handed me an old issue of *CEO Magazine*, drawing my attention to the cover story: "Travel Budgets Vs. Profit Margins: Small Firms Do the Math." I ask him what's his point, did he think I spent too much time in San Gabriel, making sure the plans were executed properly. He says, "Don't get paranoid, Ad. It's a real *inneresting* article, is all, I think you'll find it *inneresting*." Jesus!

(She has the candles lit now, and starts to blow out the match. He grabs her hand and blows for her.)

JAN *(With a sudden glint)*: I have a lot of work this weekend.

ADAM *(?)*: And no interruptions . . . I'm gone in the morning.

JAN: I mean, I have to start sooner. Rather than, you know, later.

ADAM *(Offering food)*: Care for some beef and broccoli in oyster sauce?

JAN: I can serve myself. *(Then)* Thank you, yes. *(Accepting food, smoothing the tablecloth absently)* The house feels strange without Greg.

ADAM: I wonder if everyone has these moments; they look at their wife and feel amazed at how lucky they were to land someone like her.

JAN: Is this really our first night alone in nine years? Is that possible?

ADAM *(Beat)*: So . . . what do you want to talk about?

JAN: All I can think of is Greg. How pathetic is that?

ADAM *(Playful)*: I have a topic!

JAN: Okay. Sure.

ADAM *(Offhand)*: Your nipples.

JAN *(Shocked)*: What?!!!

ADAM: We can discuss how hard they get when I lick your breasts on the side where they join your underarm—

JAN *(Shocked and aroused)*: Adam!!!

ADAM: And that little moan-gasp you make when you're aroused.

JAN: What on earth is going *on* with you . . .

ADAM: Our first night, remember the elevator?

JAN: Remember what elevator, what are you *talking* about?

ADAM: You've forgotten our first night?

JAN: What about it, what's that got to do with anyth— *(Remembers)* Oh.

ADAM: I bet that was a first for you.

JAN: Duh. Ten seconds of talk about my family, "Oh, St. Augustine, I've never been to Florida," then out of nowhere, "I love how hard your nipples get."

ADAM: It's pretty hard not to notice erect nipples when a woman has no bra on. Imagine if men stood around like that, with casual hard-ons bulging in their pants, and women were supposed to not to notice, I bet you'd get some pretty distracted conversation: "So what sort of law do you do, *is it me causing that enormous lump in your pants*, are you in corporate, did you say?" "No, I said I was a fireman, *does my aftershave make your nipples stand out like that*, but I'm taking night classes in origami, *may I suck those little puppies while we talk . . . ?*"

JAN: That's pretty much what you said.

ADAM: And you pretty much said, "Yes, thank you please."

JAN: I thought it was some hip New York pickup line; shock tactics.

(She takes a bite of her beef.)

This is really tasty.

(Adam reaches his chopsticks into another bowl. He pincers out a shrimp, and guides it suggestively toward her mouth. She reaches to guide his hand. He jerks back the chopsticks, teasing.)

ADAM: No hands.

(She opens her mouth just enough to allow the shrimp in, then clamps her teeth shut on the chopsticks, holding them tight. Their eyes lock.)

Is this a Freud moment?

JAN *(Releasing the chopsticks)*: Hmm, delicious, what's it called?

ADAM: General Wu's Golden Luck Shrimp. Also known as "*numma fie.*"

JAN *(With amused suspicion)*: Is there something about this project you haven't told me? You've been awfully frisky when you're home.

ADAM: The thing I remember most about that night, the elevator, *that* night—what I'll never forget is this one moment in the taxi—

JAN *(Cutting him short)*: Yes-yes, I'm sure. *(Then)* I still can't believe I did that. We were total strangers practically.

ADAM: What you didn't see—I've never actually mentioned this, I thought you'd be embarrassed or ashamed, which is weird considering what we did in the backseat, but at this red light when the cab was standing, a guy in this Häagen-Dazs truck next to us stared down at me with one of those New Yorky: "I-don't-even-fucking-care-you-exist-mister" expressions, and then, I guess, he must've seen your head bobbing in my lap.

JAN: Oh god, no. Someone saw?!

ADAM: His face was a riot. Total shock, then he shot me this big shit-eating grin and did this little sky punch-for-victory thing . . . and . . . I don't know what I did, probably smiled back like a dumb-ass, it doesn't matter, the point is, that moment—me with you in the back of that taxi on a hot damp night, late July, the way the city smells then: ripe garbage, body odor, stale perfume, cooking fat, the city wide open in heat, and there I am with this wild-ass babe—

JAN: "Wild-ass"? Me?

ADAM: This is true, Jan. That moment was my dream of New York. Not the office I just opened, not the bullshit puff piece about my design in Oyster Bay, nice as all that attention was, I knew it had nothing to do with me really, just media fairy dust for however long it lasted; but in that taxi with you, a casual pickup in an elevator, this healthy, all-American, hot-to-trot, foxy ex-cheerleader—

JAN: —uptight Episcopalian near-virgin . . .

ADAM: It didn't matter, my magic ruled . . . it was my own personal juju out there in the night, and no you're *right*, it was important you'd never done anything like that before, I knew that without asking and that's part of what made it so great, how I had the juice to take you so far out of yourself.

JAN: Anonymous sex with a stranger, that's what my girlfriends used to talk about and I never believed anyone could / wild nights in some faraway summer vacation land— Yugoslavia, Salzburg, Buenos Aires, and there I was, on the way to a stranger's apartment. In a taxi. Oh god—
(She remembers something)

ADAM: What?

JAN: No, it's too stupid. I can't—

ADAM *(Grins more)*: What were you about to say. Speak, woman. Stop teasing me.

JAN: What a goofbag. *(Giggling)* Is this what couples talk about when their kid has a first sleepover? Is this the typical conversation?

ADAM: You're trying to change the subject and it won't work.

(Beat. She sips her champagne.)

JAN: All right . . . and no comments.

ADAM *(Zippers lips; speaks muffled)*: Noh-ewn-ih-I-ahnedo. *["Not even if I wanted to."]*

JAN: The whole time I was / you know, back there, with you . . . The thing I worried about most—oh god, I can't . . .

ADAM: What, Jan. Tell me, please.

JAN: I was terrified we'd hit a pothole.

ADAM: "A pothole"? *(Catching on)* Ohmygod.

JAN: And we'd have to rush you to an emergency room for a, what would you even call it—

ADAM: A reattachment?

JAN: If that ever got back home! All those years, Dad wondering did I maybe scare off the "fellas" I danced with, 'cause why didn't one of them ever propose marriage?—

ADAM: Until he caught on they were, what was his expression, "A little *light in the loafers.*"

JAN: But that's not even / what I *really* worried about . . . this is serious, Adam . . . I wanted to see you again. And I was ruining it all. Men don't marry girls who jump in taxicabs with a stranger—at least not in the part of Florida where *I* grew up—which maybe explains why my friends went to Europe or South America to get nasty with a guy, but I couldn't stop myself once we started . . . I wanted to, or I wished we hadn't started, so we could say good night and exchange telephone numbers and date like normal people, and you'd take me seriously as a, a possible—lifetime mate. So I made a mini-vow—god, how crazy is this—I decided if we don't hit a pothole—

ADAM: And cause your new sex toy to need a reattachment—

JAN: Maybe then I'd have a chance with you—if you dare tell a soul about this I'll leave you, I mean it.

ADAM: I love how your mind works. Under that cool, stylish exterior you are so weird and twisted—

JAN: I couldn't believe when you called me the next afternoon. I thought you must be some kind of perv . . . and then—

ADAM: And then . . . ?

(Jan is in a kind of semi-trance.)

JAN: I realized / well, it was unbelievable, really—

ADAM: What?

JAN: You actually . . . liked me.

ADAM: More bubbles?

JAN: Even though you'd seen me out of control . . .

ADAM: At our next dinner party, when we get to the How Did You Two Meet moment, I think we should give this story a whirl.

(Adam serves her some Golden Luck Shrimp.)

JAN *(Beat)*: This feels very weird, Adam.

ADAM: Being alone together?

JAN: Talking about . . . like this, these things.

ADAM: Why?

JAN: How we've been lately. Since I started the business . . . and you got this project in the Midwest . . . I mean things were bad. We both know it. But now, when you're home suddenly it's all champagne, romantic dinner, and now sexy talk. Isn't it strange that things improve like this when you're not around so much? Have you noticed?

ADAM: We used to be like this all the time.

JAN: When?

ADAM: At the beginning.

JAN: Before Greg.

ADAM: Whoa, don't lay this on Greg, we were all over each other long after Greg, every morning when the school bus picked him up, into the bedroom like two rabbits / this is not about Greg, when we *wanted to be close*, we were close.

JAN: Tim's call—he was worried the last few times you were out of town he couldn't reach you. Your room didn't answer.

ADAM: Oh. *That's* what this is all about.

JAN: He wondered if I'd managed to get through . . .

ADAM: Stop it, Jan. You know half the time I forget I plugged the computer in the phone jack. He knows my cell phone number if it's that important.

JAN *(Beat)*: So why'd he call me about it?

(Adam pushes his chair back from the table.)

ADAM: Why don't you ask him?

JAN: I'm asking *you*.

ADAM: Okay, educated guess. What does Tim know about us? (A) That you think he's an obnoxious, untalented loudmouth who conned me into a partnership, and you make no effort to conceal your feelings when we're together and, (B) our marriage was going through a rough patch. Well, what better way to stir things up than a call suggesting maybe I'm out all night with some bimbo, which will—if you don't take a minute to think it through—may start a huge blowup Chez Penzius, and with a little luck we'll end up divorced, just like him, and he'll have his revenge on you, and level the playing field with his old buddy-partner-fellow-architect, who then becomes just another middle-aged divorced guy with an angry ex-wife, fucked-up children and major regrets about his whole life. Would be my guess.

(Suddenly she's in tears, rising from the table to get a tissue from the island.)

JAN: It's been a very hard time, Adam. Very hard.

ADAM: I know that.

JAN: I don't think so. I don't think you really understand the pressure I'm under.

ADAM: Not specifically, but I see the time it takes—

JAN: It's not the time, I don't mind that. It's the crookedness. Every database I buy is nine-tenths garbage; they unload junk lists on me, out of date, inaccurate—and it's just how business is done, everyone's trying to fuck everyone else for a buck, and I feel so . . . naive and sheltered. All I know about is home, where we treat each other decently, where I'm in this zone of civilized behavior.

ADAM: Speaking of nipples— *(He starts toward her)*

JAN *(Waves him away)*: Is everything just a big joke to you?

ADAM: It's just something I don't want between us tonight.

JAN: Well I don't either, but I can't make it go away. I can't pretend Greg isn't watching me like a hungry dog every time I look up from my work, poor monkey. And you, wanting my company. I can't just set my work aside like knitting. I'm trained as a dancer for pete's sake, not a database manipulator. It's a very steep learning curve and you haven't been very understanding— *(She almost cries again)*

(Adam starts toward her. She waves him away.)

I know how stressed I've been. And I—I feel so badly.

(He holds her.)

ADAM: We've been through worse. We'll survive.

JAN *(Vulnerable)*: Sometimes I wonder.

(He pours champagne.)

ADAM: Drink. Relax. Let me serve you. Then we'll go upstairs and make love all night.

(She sips.)

JAN *(In her own thoughts)*: Thank god Greg found a friend. He's so afraid of everything, so / his little rituals . . . he counts his footsteps wherever he goes, I hear him, you know—under his breath: one, two, three, four . . . and if he loses count he walks back to where he was and starts all over again. That can't be normal behavior.

(Adam massages her shoulders. She stiffens.)

What are you do—

ADAM *(Silences her)*: Shhh, relax . . . I'm untying your back. Breathe deep.
JAN: I'll have to be up very very early, Adam.
ADAM: Do that dancer exercise, make your mind blank.
JAN: Promise you'll talk to him about the hamster.
ADAM: I promise.
JAN: And the map.
ADAM: I will.
JAN: Don't just say it, Adam.
ADAM: There is no stress in Brooklyn tonight. It's hot, it's damp, we're in the back of a taxi—
JAN: Oh that feels so good. Right there . . . higher, higher . . . to the left. Yeeeesss.

(He slides his hand inside her blouse. She leans back against his arm, moaning as the lights fade.)

Yes. Like that. Oh, yes.

(Scene change:

    Adam mounts the stairs anticipating what lies ahead.

    The lights grow dim on stage—not quite realistic. Time passes.

    Jan rises languorously, blows out the candles and starts for the stairway. The laptop catches her eye. She opens it without any real intention, but data on the screen holds her focus. There's a detail that's wrong. She begins to correct a few numbers, spreading her paperwork beside her laptop, growing lost in the task at hand.

    The clock reads: 11:55 P.M.

    The lights come up on:)

SCENE 2

Jan sits at one end of the table, briefcase and laptop open, paperwork spread out, dishes still on the table.

Adam descends the stairs in a bathrobe. He sees her absorbed in her work. She is unaware of him.

He removes an open bottle of white wine from the fridge and slams the door shut.

Jan yelps, clutches her chest, startled.

JAN: Adam, don't do that, god!

(She calms herself.)

ADAM: I was getting wine.
JAN *(Irritated)*: I didn't hear you come in. Don't sneak around, please.
ADAM: Wine?

JAN: Oh. Thank you, yes. *(She pays little attention as she holds out her glass)* Pour it in here . . .

(He does. He stands there. She works.)

(Being patient) I'm trying to finish this, sweetie.

ADAM: I went to take a shower—while you cleaned up down here.

JAN: I'm sorry . . . what?

ADAM: Nothing.

JAN: I have to finish this one category, then— *(Sweetly)* I'll just be a minute.

ADAM: Do you know what time it is?

JAN: Time? Why?

ADAM: Almost midnight.

JAN *(Sinking in)*: Oh.

ADAM: My hair's already dry.

JAN: I must've lost track of . . .

ADAM: Two hours.

JAN: Oh, sweetie, I'm sorry. *(Her work)* —I'll be right up, okay? I'm on lawyers, it's a major list—

ADAM: I'm being unreasonable, right? We start making love over dinner, we're really getting into it, I rush upstairs to shower while you clear the table, and after waiting in bed for two hours I get all, I don't know, impatient and irritable . . .

JAN: I said I was sorry. I'll be right with you.

ADAM: This doesn't compute for you, does it? The *strangeness* of your behavior.

JAN: I want to be relaxed when we / I don't want my mind on other things.

ADAM: If you'd come upstairs when we started making love, when your mind was, it looked like, very much on nothing except . . . me.

(Beat.)

JAN: I apologize. Give me five minutes.

(Beat.)

ADAM: You know what? You finish up here. Take your time. I'll go to bed. And when I get back home Wednesday we'll sit down together with our diaries and find a mutually convenient time to copulate.

JAN: Oh, Adam, don't be childish.

ADAM: Good night.

(He turns to go.)

JAN: Adam?!

ADAM: What?!

JAN: I'm—sorry. I need this for tomorrow afternoon, an important client. I lost track of time.

ADAM: Great!

JAN: This is so typical, you know. You whip up a new agenda for the marriage and expect me to drop everything and jump aboard—I don't have time, Adam, not since I started having to squeeze thirty hours of work into a twenty-four-hour day . . .

ADAM *(Biting)*: I guess if I didn't have more to do all week than sit around fantasizing about my wife's erect nipples, trying to figure out how to get her in bed. If I maybe had a business to run with eleven employees, and a semi-alcoholic partner, and a son to bring to school each day, and a home to pay for, and breakfast to make for my kid, and lunch to pack for him, and shopping for dinner, maybe I'd appreciate better the pressure you're under day and night—

JAN: I hate when you do that calm sarcastic thing.

ADAM: That's a criticism, right? So I'm, let's see, impatient, not very understanding, and calmly sarcastic. Let me get some paper and start a list . . .

JAN *(Abrupt)*: You want to make love? Fine, we'll make love.

(She closes her folder with a childish flourish.)

ADAM: Whoops. I just came. Sorry, darling, you're such a turn-on.

JAN: You are so fucking lame, Adam.

ADAM: There was a time when you didn't think so.

JAN: Just go to bed if you're going to be like this . . .

ADAM: Go fuck yourself. No one else will.

(He storms upstairs. She sips some wine. Adam returns.)

You know, when you withdraw like this behind a veil of irritation—all the things I want to say to you, tell you, explain . . . they just—I end up so fucking furious I can't stand being in the same house as you. That's how it starts, you know, these standoffs, these weeks of shouldering past each other in the hall, I hate it, I fucking hate feeling so shut out—never mind not making love, I don't even want to touch you. How can you survive for so long without / don't you need contact?

JAN: Other things have to come first right now.

ADAM: How long is *right now*? Ballpark figure: one week, one year, when Greg graduates from college?

JAN: I need you to be a grown-up, Adam. I can't deal with two children in this house, I need an adult to share the burden.

ADAM *(Beat)*: We're firing half our office.

(She takes a moment to figure out what he's referring to . . . the shift is so sudden.)

JAN *(Listening)*: Since when?

ADAM: Not enough business.

JAN: I thought you were branching out. Isn't this Midwest project a whole new market, I thought you said.

ADAM: Not so much a market, more—it's desperation. Lowering our sights.

JAN: You've had dry spells before.

(She sighs. It looks like she won't be able to avoid this one.)

Why is this any different?

ADAM: We're four months behind on the office rent. We have to sublet everything but the top-floor annex.

JAN: Well, you started there. You were fine.

ADAM: That was eighteen years ago, Jan. I was young. I was hot. I had a style, *something* that passed for a style, something distinctive enough to create demand for my work, and right now all I have is a partner who not only doesn't care about the quality of our output, he'd be happy if we were in-house architects for the Mormon Church, he's jumping up and down about winning a contract from the city, renovating public toilets in Van Cortlandt Park . . .

JAN: Oh, come on, sweetie, things are always up and down in your field; nature of the beast, that's what you always tell me.

ADAM: I tell you that because I don't want to worry you, okay? Because you grew up with sunshine and navel oranges and money everywhere and never had to learn what it means to be facing complete ruin. I tell you because I don't think you can handle the truth about being on the brink of bankruptcy, about to watch the city marshals carry your furniture out the door—these are things you thank god you never had to witness growing up, and I'm telling you now because, for the first time ever, I'm just not sure I have the will to drag my firm back out of the hole one more time. I'm tired of never reaching a place where I can rest.

JAN: Oh, dear, someone's had a bad day.

ADAM: Tim wasn't always a burnout. He had ambitions. He was a damn good architect. Now he's / toilets in Van Cortlandt . . . and me, an industrial park in a soybean field.

JAN: One day you're a dancer, then . . . you're a mom with a house to look after, and laundry, and recycling—so you peddle data to online marketers. That's the breaks.

ADAM: I guess it is.

JAN *(Almost without thought)*: Oh, Adam, I wish you were— *(Stops)*

ADAM *(Beat)*: You wish I was *what?*

JAN: Never mind.

ADAM: Let's skip the almost-say-it-then-withhold routine? You wish I was what? Taller? Not so worried about money? Frank Lloyd Wright? Frank Gehry? Anyone called Frank?

JAN *(Direct)*: I wish you were tougher.

ADAM *(Beat)*: Tougher.

JAN: Stronger, yes. A stronger person.

(He lets this sink in. He looks calm, but is stung.)

ADAM: The thing is, to win the hand of a-man-with-the-balls-you-wish-I-had, wouldn't you have to have some small amount of sexual allure as a woman?

JAN: Touché. We're even.

ADAM: Would you like to know what I wish?

JAN *(Tired of this)*: *What*, Adam.

ADAM: I wish you weren't such a withholding, anxious, critical bitch.

JAN: *ADAM!!!* Okay, you want this, you want to know what I'm dealing with here?

ADAM: Actually, I just want to go to bed.

JAN: You started it.

ADAM: What "it"? I tried to make love to you, I tried to get close—

JAN: This wasn't the time.

ADAM: When, Janine, when *will* it be?

JAN: I don't know. Soon. When my business is working. When a lot of lowlife dot.com scumbags aren't selling me bogus data. Next week. Later tonight. But not right this minute. Why do you have to care so much, why does everything have to depend on my readiness to get laid, why am I *so important.* You have this magical idea about family, like it's this eternal Disney World where everyone's smiling and warm and available 24-7. It's twisted, Adam. And it's beginning to not be a convincing excuse that you didn't grow up in one. When it's working, family's a nice thing, but when it's not, it's hell, and that's how it stays until it gets good again. Tonight's a down. This month, this year, is a down. There'll be worse to come, I promise you. And we'll get through it if you'll allow things to be difficult, if you understand sometimes I'm a cunt, and sometimes you're a pathetic childish asshole, and it's just no big deal, okay?

ADAM: I wish I knew what to do with you.

(They laugh.)

JAN: I'll drink to that.

(She holds her glass out. He pours.)

All right. I was saving this for when you came back, but we might as well deal with it.

(She finally pushes all her paperwork away.)

The school called.

(He hesitates just a moment.)

ADAM: Why?

JAN: Greg. Another incident.

ADAM: Incident? Oh, like him breaking those pencils? Is this being upgraded from classroom mischief to a full-scale "incident"?

JAN: Carole Bonibeaux wants us to come in next week.

ADAM: Why?

JAN: She's concerned about Greg.

ADAM: She's the school shrink, whipping up things to be concerned about is what she's paid to do. If she doesn't find some fly-shit in the pepper, she's out of work. *(Beat)* What did Greg do? That caused concern?

JAN: He disappeared.

ADAM: Into thin air?

JAN: They searched the school building. They thought he ran away. They were about to call the police when the janitor found him hiding under a pile of clothing in Lost and Found. He'd taken everything off the hangers and made a nest or something in the corner. I got the call at lunch. I had to leave a client.

ADAM: Why is a prank like that relegated to the school shrink?

JAN: There's some concern that Greg might have a problem.

ADAM: A problem.

JAN: Maybe at home, that's what Ms. Bonibeaux— He could be reacting to some change in domestic routine . . . My return to work . . . your travel.

ADAM: Maybe he's just hiding under a pile of clothes.

JAN: That's what she wants to look into.

ADAM: I bet she does. Ms. Boney-Butt with her symptom-finder takes aim at the parents . . . oooh, Mommy's back at work and ooooh, Daddy's on the road. Jesus Fucking Christ—

JAN: Are you done?

ADAM: She's not, that's for damn sure.

JAN: She suggested we should think about getting him tested.

ADAM: Did she. And what shrinky colleague-friend of hers would she recommend to do the actual testing for how much money plus a referral fee?

JAN: Sweetie, Greg zones out in class, he never completes assignments; they're not convinced he can handle fifth grade next year.

ADAM: Well this may sound like a radical idea, but why not put him into fifth grade and find out!

JAN: Something about his behavior concerns them. That's all.

ADAM: You know when they should start to worry, when he sets fire to a classroom. When he puts poison in the chemistry teacher's coffee to see what effect it has, when he pushes bicycles into oncoming traffic because he loves to hear screeching tires, when he has sex with a one-armed basketball coach—when he does any of these things, or all of them, they should maybe get a *little* concerned, and at that point I'll pay them a visit and reassure them that I did all of those things myself in my wayward youth, only I was lucky enough to not have experts around deciding it was something more than it was: childhood in this wondrous republic of ours.

JAN: This is not your life, it's Greg's. You didn't want him to grow up like you in any way. Fine, Penrose Academy is not an arty-farty develop-the-inner-child alternate school like yours, it's an actual accredited institution that teaches an actual curriculum, and if they're worried about Greg—

ADAM: He's a kid. Not all behavior is a symptom, sometimes behavior's just . . . behavior. Leave him alone.

JAN: He may have problems.

ADAM: Because Ms. Bone-the-Butt says so?

JAN: She's the school shrink.

ADAM: Jan, what's going on? We've explored this at painful lengths, remember? School shrinks are the bottom of the therapeutic food chain. So Ms. Boney-Butt lucked into a cushy private school, good for her, may she never have to find a real job, the only question is: *Why allow her to even register on your radar?*

JAN *(A little drifty)*: She does have awful teeth. And who does her hair?!

ADAM: There's our response: "Sorry, Ms. Bonney LaButt, but in our household we eschew the council of all bony-ass skanks with rotten teeth and bad hair."

JAN: What about his homework? And he has no friends his own age, well maybe Joey now, but there's the zoning out. And what about fifth grade? And why would he hide under clothing?

ADAM: 'Cause he's a hamster? 'Cause it's fun? And no more worrisome than a ballerina who even at a very advanced stage of her maturing process sucks off strangers in the backseat of a taxi—

JAN: Those are two completely unrelated things.

ADAM: Maybe it's a social protest—have you seen the clothes in the Penrose Lost and Found?—four-hundred-dollar designer jackets, kids just drop them in the courtyard— maybe Greg was making a statement, *"Look how I can build an entire shelter out of what you don't even care enough to look after?"*

JAN *(Waivering)*: Maybe all the fuss *is* a little premature. *(More gently)* It's funny . . . when you put things the way you do—

ADAM: In that un-tough, wimpy way of mine?

JAN: Half the time when you're around I just want you out of my hair. —When you're gone, I need you. What *is* that?

ADAM: I don't know. Maybe you should be tested.

JAN *(Arms out, cutesy-helpless)*: Hug.

(An affectionate hug. Then Adam gets his wine.)

ADAM: This must be the fight we have when I'm going on the road. I thought we had it over dinner. We had a delayed fight.

JAN: Greg seems all right to you? His behavior?

ADAM *(Beat)*: Yes, you *are* a wonderful mother.

JAN: What?

ADAM: Isn't that what you're worried about—

JAN *(Smiles)*: I hate how well you know me.

(She kicks off her shoes, looks around feeling sexy and flirtatious.)

Was I really working just before? While you were waiting upstairs all stiff and eager? What is *wrong* with me? Pour some wine.

(He obeys, but pours only a little.)

More. I am a good mom, you know. I yell, I ride Greg, and you, and I worry too much, but compared to some . . . which of course I'd never do, but if I did . . . And I'm pretty attractive, you have to admit. Doormen still give me the eye, you know. And I do love you, Adam. I mean, the whole deal. Like we were just before. And like we are now. And in a bunch of other ways that probably haven't even happened yet. It's a stupid word: "love." There should be fifty words for it, like Eskimos have for snow. Go on, I'll be right up.

ADAM: I'm not leaving you alone down here with all this sexy data. *You* first. I'll be right behind your tush. Watching it ascend the stairway. Step by swaying step.

(They kiss, familiar, easy. She closes a folder and is about to pop it in her briefcase when she sees a scribble . . .)

JAN *(Trying to remember)*: Oh, here, I forgot . . . a call, some woman from, I didn't recognize the area code: "Will call office," I wrote. No message.

ADAM *(A bit tense)*: When was this?

JAN: 'Round nine. She sounded frazzled. *(Joking)* Didn't she know you were married?

ADAM *(With studied easiness)*: Any other messages?

JAN *(Beat)*: What's her name? *(Looking at him intently now)* I was joking, sweetie. It's someone's secretary, right? *(Beat)* Isn't it?

ADAM *(Recovering; new joke)*: I'd never give a mistress my home number. *(He's smooth, but a line's been crossed)*

JAN *(Focused)*: What's her name, Adam? *(Beat)* Tell me her name?

(She waits. Beat.
  Scene change:
  The lights dim slightly as Jan wanders to the fridge and opens it. The light from inside the fridge throws her into a silhouette. She stands motionless in the light. Time passes.
  Adam sits at the table, watching her.
  The clock reads: 12:19 A.M.
  The lights come up on:)

SCENE 3

Adam watches and waits. Jan, in her bare feet, remains dazed, motionless, bent into the light from the open fridge.

ADAM: I'm sorry. *(Beat)* Jan . . . I'm sorry.

(*She doesn't move.*)

What are you looking for?

(*Beat.*)

Janine?

(*Beat.*)

Did you hear me? Neen?

(She spins and screams, snatching random items from the fridge, hurling them blindly in his direction.)

JAN: YOU *SHIT*, YOU FUCKING *SHIT*, YOU *BASTARD* FUCKING LIAR COWARDLY *SHIT*—

ADAM: Jan!

JAN *(Throws; he ducks)*: FUCKING FILTHY HORRIBLE WEAK-WILLED MOTHER*FUCKER*—

(She throws a jar at him. It shatters all over the dining room.)

ADAM: Stop it, STOP IT, JAN—

JAN: DON'T TELL ME TO STOP, *(Throws)* YOU DON'T GET TO TELL ME ANYTHING EVER AGAIN, YOU BETRAYING FUCKING BETRAYER.

(He grabs her.)

ADAM: Stop!!!

(She shakes free.)

JAN: I WILL NOT STOP, I WILL NOT, NOT, I'LL HURT YOU—I'll hurt you so badly, get away from me, please just leave me alone.

ADAM: You should sit down.

JAN: You have no right to live.

(She wanders to the table, distraught; hurt and confusion slowly replacing anger.)

ADAM: What?

JAN: Oh, fuck. Fuck, fuck, fuck—

ADAM: What happened?

JAN: Glass . . .

ADAM: Sit down.

JAN: Stay away. *(The culprit underfoot)* The jar, Jesus!!!

(She tries to walk, but it hurts. She sits.)

There's glass in my foot. I told you not to put glass containers in the front of the fridge. Don't just stand there, Adam, get a bandage, get the first-aid kit.

(He goes to find it.)

I said get the—

ADAM: I am. It's in the bathroom—

JAN: That's not where we keep / don't you know where anything is in this house? What if Greg got hurt? How can you not know where to find the first-aid kit?

ADAM *(Beat)*: It's in the medicine cabinet in the corner of the bathroom.

JAN: We haven't kept it there for over a year. Didn't you notice I'd reorganized the bathroom?

ADAM *(Patient and angry all at once)*: Just tell me where the first-aid kit is.

JAN: Where do you think it is, it's where I put it, on the top shelf of the cupboard. What's the point of keeping it in the bathroom when we spend most of our life in the kitchen.

ADAM *(With fierce control)*: You didn't tell me. I didn't know.

(She looks at the bottom of her bloody foot. Adam brings over the first-aid kit.)

JAN: Give it to me. I'll deal with my foot, you sweep the glass.

(Adam ignores her, preparing a cotton ball with alcohol.)

Adam, sweep the glass.

ADAM: Shut up.

JAN: What?

ADAM: I said shut up. I'm cleaning your foot. When I'm finished cleaning your foot, then I'll sweep the glass.

(He takes her foot. She pulls it away. He grabs it again. This time she lets him hold her foot.)

JAN: Don't talk to me like that.

ADAM: Like what?

JAN: Rude. You can't be rude to me after what you did—

ADAM: I should be on the defensive, as usual? Is that it?

JAN *(She winces as the cotton touches her wound)*: Owww, careful.

ADAM: It has to be clean so I can see the glass. Just hold still. It'll sting, I can't help that.

(Jan sits motionless while he bathes her foot.)

JAN: Why did you— *(She stops)*

ADAM: Finish the question.

JAN: Why did you cheat on me.

ADAM *(Beat)*: Because— Do you really want to know? Isn't it enough that I, I—

JAN: *Betrayed* me. Me and Greg?

ADAM *(Stops cleaning)*: Greg?

JAN: I thought that's what this was all about, this marriage— this life we chose—to make a family, like you never had.

ADAM: That's what we've done.

JAN: Wasn't that the attraction of someone like me, god knows we had nothing else in common, but there was my Sunkist all-American sitcom Florida background. Greg's guaranteed at least one set of normal grandparents, with truckloads of healthy cousins and aunts and uncles.

What happened to your fucking Hallmark Greeting Card
family when that bitch spread her legs? . . .

ADAM: How does what I told you change any of—

JAN: Now he's just another kid from a broken home. No big
deal, I guess. Most of the students at that snotty-ass
school are the same.

ADAM: How did we arrive at a broken home? You want a divorce?

JAN: It's not what I *want*, no; I want to continue being what
I thought we were when I came home tonight, a married
couple going through a bad patch—back in the days when
I thought you had the strength to handle my bad stuff
without racing into the arms of whoever for comfort.

ADAM *(Beat)*: Do you want to know why I did it?

JAN: No. The last thing I want is to understand your actions,
to see your side of things and sympathize. Jesus!

(Adam stops what he's doing.)

Is the glass out?

ADAM: You just asked, no started to ask, why I slept with her.
Which is it, do you want to know or not?

JAN *(Steely)*: Did you get out the glass?

ADAM *(With bitter glee)*: And the answer is—you *want* to
know, and you *don't* want to know. And that, in a nutshell,
is the story of our marriage. You want one thing, and you
want its opposite. Spend more time with Greg. Then,
stop spoiling him, he can be alone for an hour. Or, "*Why
do you work all the time and leave me to do everything
at home,*" then, "*Why don't you go after more clients so
we can afford someone to clean the house,*" or—look at
your face, it's actually / you're smiling, no it's a smirk,
a triumphant— You've been vindicated, I did the thing
you live for; I wronged you. I betrayed the family you
sacrificed your career for. You've been crowned the Queen
of Unfair. You should thank me.

JAN *(Shaken by this)*: I had no idea you were so angry.

ADAM *(Growing immediately calmer, his tirade stops)*: I didn't either.

JAN: Could you finish with my foot? Please?

(He starts examining her foot, cleaning it again.)

Who is she?

ADAM: Someone I used to know. A long time ago.

JAN: Were you intimate—a long time ago.

ADAM: We had a / we were intimate.

JAN: Before . . . *us?*

ADAM: Yes. Before we married.

JAN: That's not what I asked. We lived together eight years. Was it during then?

ADAM: Yes.

JAN *(Hurt)*: But—we were happy. I thought / weren't we happy?

ADAM: We lived separate lives.

JAN: You wanted that. We were . . . getting established. I danced, you architected, we gave each other space. *(Regarding her foot)* See anything?

ADAM: Hold still.

JAN: Isn't that what you wanted . . . independence?

ADAM: Until she happened.

JAN: Then why didn't you go off with her. When it was simple. Before we had this whole messy life together. Before Greg.

ADAM: It wasn't about that. We didn't really know each other. We didn't talk. It was just intense sex. Anonymous . . . intense . . . I-don't-know-what-exactly it was.

(He finds the glass piece.)

There. Raise your foot slowly. Hold still.

(He takes up tweezers.)

JAN: You frighten me, Adam. We're so different.

ADAM: And she was married. Two young kids.

JAN: Wonderful, a married woman!

ADAM: A prominent family where they live.

JAN *(Beat)*: If she wasn't married, would you have—

ADAM: It wasn't about marriage; it wasn't about love, it wasn't really even about sex.

JAN: I'm trying to think what that leaves.

ADAM: Intimacy . . . closeness—

JAN: A married person with two children. *(Beat)* She's out there? Where you go? On these trips?

ADAM: Yes.

JAN: And you see her every time you—

ADAM: I was about to—end it. This trip.

JAN: And why's that?

ADAM: It wasn't what we thought. It got complicated. She's not where my life is. *(Pulls out glass sliver)* Got it!

(He holds up the piece of glass.)

Shall I bandage?

(He starts to work. She watches him.)

JAN: I don't know what we are now. What are we?

ADAM: Do you know, whenever I try and touch you, you flinch.

JAN: I don't flinch.

ADAM: It's reflex. Any contact, you recoil. Every meal turns into a fight, and by the time we've finished eating the tension is so / sex is out of the question. You end up down here working. I read, watch TV. You just can't bear the thought of letting anything past this wall around you, least of all your husband.

JAN: Then make me.

ADAM: What, force myself on you?

JAN: If that's what it takes.

ADAM *(Half joking)*: You want me to ravage you?

JAN: I want to know that you want me more than anything in the world. I want you to stop being complicated, make your demands known, and let me say a simple yes or no.

ADAM: You hate it when I impose myself—

JAN: I hate how you approach halfway, then linger on the sidelines all patient and kind, watching out for my needs. Being *sensitive* to me. All that touchy-feely awareness, I hate how much you notice me, how you wait for me to make the first move, why can't you just—like that night in the taxi, come after me, you know, yes, ravage me, give me no choice for christ sake—

ADAM: You hate that.

JAN: So what? I love it, too. You fly a thousand miles to fuck this married woman, why can't you make the same effort for me, risk me, risk my saying no, risk my anger, my resistance. For once in your life take me on and win me.

(They exchange a long look. He moves to kiss her.)

What are you—

ADAM: Don't move.

JAN: Not now, I didn't mean right . . . now—

(She struggles against him, but he kisses her.)

You can't just—I meant, in general.

(He keeps moving in on her.)

It's too late, Adam. You should have done this without my having to tell you.

ADAM: I've never wanted anyone else in the world since / but you won't give yourself to me, okay, if this is how you want it—

JAN: Stop, Adam!!!

ADAM: Shut up.

(He slaps her.)

JAN *(Stunned)*: Adam!!!

ADAM *(Horrified at himself)*: Oh god, Jan, I'm so—

JAN: Don't say anything . . .

(She responds by grabbing him. For a moment it seems like rage, then it becomes a wild, desperate sexual encounter. She cries with pain.)

My foot, oh jesus, it hurts, sweetie . . . Just let me / a painkiller, anything, pleeease . . .

ADAM: No. Right now.

(She succumbs eagerly, with noises and gasps . . . They move onto the table . . . he sweeps data charts onto the floor.)

JAN: What are we doing, this isn't us . . .

(The telephone rings. Both freeze.)

ADAM: Let it ring.

JAN: It might be Greg.

ADAM: Fuck him, he can get through the night alone.

(The machine clicks on: "It's Jan and Adam, we can't get to the phone right now, but leave a message at the beep and we'll call you back . . . Beep." Then Mrs. Pelligrini speaks with some alarm:)

MRS. PELLIGRINI *(Lilting Italian accent)*: Hello? Hello? Is somebody there, please, I'm calling about Gregory, please . . .

(Jan races to the phone and picks up.)

JAN: Mrs. Pelligrini, is everything okay? *(Beat)* Oh. Good. I thought you were—you sounded . . . *(Beat)* No, it's okay . . . it's just . . . so late . . . *(Beat)* They should have been asleep hours ago. *(Beat)* They are? *(Beat)* Good, I'm so glad. *(Beat)* Yeah, well, you know, Greg talks about Joey all the time, too. *(Beat; puzzled)* Yeah . . . Un-huh. Is there something you needed to talk about . . . *(Beat)* Oh. Ummm, yeah, I guess that would be . . . *(She cups the phone and explains to Adam)* She and her husband want to take the boys to Six Flags Adventure Park tomorrow. Is that okay? *(Into the phone)* Oh, wait a minute, he has a project due on Monday— *(She stops)*

(Adam is gesturing to her, "Give him a break.")

(Into the phone) Okay! *(Then)* No, no, we don't need to speak to him, just *(Beat)* I'm sorry, they what? Fell asleep / *Oh*, in front of the TV, okay, I didn't under— So this is your idea? *(Beat)* No, it's great they're having such a good time together . . . Well, thank you very much. We'll expect you around six. Okay, "*Grazia.*" *(She hangs up)*
(Bemused) The kids want to spend tomorrow together.

(Adam approaches. His intentions are clear. He starts to kiss her. She gently pushes him back.)

We have to talk.
ADAM: Later.

(He kisses her.)

JAN: This isn't what I meant. Adam, we can't—not after . . . this is too strange.

(He continues to kiss her, leading her slowly upstairs.)

It won't change anything. Do you understand? *(Starting to succumb)* Why now, Adam. Why didn't you do this before . . . Why did you need someone else? Why wasn't I . . . enough?

(The stage is empty. The lights grow dim.
 Scene change:
 Jan descends the stairs in a nightdress, weak and wobbly-kneed from milestone sex.
 She carries a heavy valise, which she sets on the table. She sees Adam's T-shirt from when they started making love. She folds it, packs it in the valise, and sets the valise by the front door.
 She takes a long drink of water, refills the glass, and carries it to the table.
 She collects her disheveled papers, sits in front of her laptop, and starts to work.
 The clock reads: 3:10 A.M.
 The lights come up on:)

SCENE 4

Adam descends the stairs in boxers and a T-shirt. Jan glances up briefly, a lazy distant smile. The mood is postcoital.

ADAM: Work?

JAN *(Casually)*: Final edits. Tomorrow's my big dot.com client. *(Seeing her watch)* Today, actually; later today. How do you do it, how do you sell yourself?

ADAM: Pretend it's a performance; dance for them.

JAN: I can't blow this. I need a *"yes"* from somewhere.

ADAM: Wasn't what just happened upstairs enough "yes" to hold you?

(Her look unsettles him.)

What? *(She looks back at her work)* You want cinnamon toast? I made some fresh spread for Greg.

JAN *(Good-humored)*: More sugar. Just what he needs.

(He sits.)

ADAM: It's amazing two people can be together for so long and still have something like that happen. That was / well, I knew you were amazing, but *that* amazing?

JAN: Mnnn.

ADAM: Am I interrupting?

JAN *(Shaking her head no)*: It's all right.

(He puts his hand on hers and squeezes. She looks at him with a faraway smile. Her calm is too calm.)

ADAM: I was thinking about Greg—

JAN *(Pointedly)*: I *would* like some cinnamon toast. Write down the recipe, yes. Greg loves it, doesn't he?

(Adam is happy to have a task. He goes to make toast, grabbing a small plastic container of his mix.)

ADAM: It's just margarine and brown sugar and cinnamon. I don't actually measure the proportions. I just mix them together until the color looks right—

JAN: It's so strange that you should bring up that taxi ride tonight, of all nights—

ADAM: I guess we're still on the same wavelength—

JAN: —because, you know, adding everything up, Tim's phone call, your recent behavior, it did occur to me that you were fucking someone else. That all this sex talk, at our time of life, it might be spillover from someone else's warm bath—no, darling, it's okay. I'm not angry. More intrigued. Connections, you know. How you called me up after the taxi ride, wanted to see me, seemed not to be bothered by my dirty stuff . . .

ADAM: It wasn't dirty, Jan. Nothing about you is . . .

JAN: Oh yeah, it is. The tip of the iceberg as it turns out. But I'm beginning to see how that whole idea of being able to share things with a stranger . . . like my friends in Europe—how you can say just about anything to a person when you know there's no future.

ADAM: Jan?

JAN: No, it's nice, really. Too bad you can't have this all the time in a marriage. A new husband every night. Someone you'll never see again. I feel like I can tell you anything right now.

ADAM: Jan, I'm not sure where this is going.

JAN: The marriage, you mean? It's going nowhere. It's over. It's gone.

ADAM: After what just happened?

JAN: What "*just happened*?" Are we talking about your year-and-whatever fuckfest in the Midwest? Your months and months of betrayal, and I'm not counting the early days with her when you and me were supposedly in love—

ADAM: I mean tonight. Between the two of us.

JAN: Because we smacked each other around? Got a little violent. Lifted the veil an inch or two on our little beasties?

ADAM: Okay, it frightened me, too, but at least something's out in the open now—

JAN: God, Adam, you're such a shameless self-deceiver. I see how this is falling together in your mind. You fucked some other woman, repeatedly, over years, but the wonderful thing is, it somehow led to a buffo act of life-altering sex that brought you and your wife closer and enriched our marriage, isn't life a mysterious and wondrous thing, blah-blah, some arty-ass garbage like that?

ADAM: No. I'm aware this changes things.

JAN: How does it change them. How, Adam!

ADAM: I'll have to win back your trust.

JAN: Oh god, can't you think of something within reason?

ADAM: This is wild talk, Jan, I'm lost.

JAN (*Quieter now, referring to the valise*): I repacked your valise. There's enough for your trip and a week or so

125

more. When you fly back, find yourself a hotel room.
I don't want you here.

(He goes to the valise.)

ADAM: What's this?

JAN: It'll be easier on all of us . . . We'll meet up mid-week,
after we've both had time to think more about arrangements for the future.

ADAM *(Flabbergasted)*: You're not serious.

JAN *(Deadly serious)*: Look at me, Adam. Do you see any sign
of levity?

ADAM: What was that all about just before, upstairs?

JAN: It was a fantastic, weird, scary, unbelievably wonderful
fuck. I'll remember it fondly.

ADAM: I'm sorry, you can't do this. No.

JAN: I am. I'm doing it. What else did you think was happening?

ADAM: I thought—we were working it out.

JAN: Working *what* out? You just violated the contract. Rob
a bank, go to jail. Betray your family, lose it. Or did you
forget that part of the ceremony that goes "forsaking all
others," which I understand to mean—

ADAM: I know what it means . . .

JAN: You have no idea, Adam. You couldn't possibly understand
or you'd have never dared tell me what you did.

ADAM: Is that the crime? That I told you?

JAN: How else would I have known?

ADAM: You want me to have secrets from you?

JAN: I'm your wife, of course I want you to have secrets from
me. If I can't trust you to shut up about your infidelities,
what on earth *can* I trust you for?

ADAM: You're really spooky.

JAN: No, Adam. I'm normal. I'm what normal people are
like. You think my mom sounds crazy, you should meet
some of her St. Augustine club ladies. "Pillows of the

Community" they call themselves. Charming wives and mothers, but just under the surface they're all loony-tunes, most of them from pretending all those years to be happy wives and mothers. But do you think they'd ever up and ruin everyone's life by blabbing the truth. They don't call little Jimmy in the kitchen and say, "You're a spoiled ungrateful drain on this family, and dealing with your incessant demands has caused me and my husband to fall out of love with each other, so why don't you take this one-way ticket to Bhutan and stay there until you're financially independent and able to do your own laundry." And they don't tell their poor hubbies, "Honey, you were always kind of boring and predictable but you're becoming a sort of parody of yourself lately, plus you're putting on weight which is very unappealing, and I hate that aftershave you use, not to mention the things I learn about your digestive system when I do the wash." No, we don't say these things, we drink some wine and we smile, and we expect our husbands to act with the same restraint, and refrain from telling us when you're fucking other women, we do not want to know that: Too Much Information, Do Not Share, thank you.

ADAM: You want me to *lie*? Is that what you're saying?

JAN: I want you to call a car service and leave.

ADAM: My flight's not till nine. I'm not going anywhere till then.

JAN: *Now*, Adam.

ADAM: I'll be upstairs.

JAN: I put 9-1-1 on autodial. Don't make me use it.

ADAM: Let's just calm down and talk this through.

JAN: I'm not your friend anymore. We're back in that taxi, but this time you didn't get lucky with a well-raised girl on a Big City Adventure, this time I'm a real New York story, babe, a crazy bitch who bites it off and spits it out the window and steals your wallet and leaves you with herpes. Get used to it, 'cause this safe little world I built for you just fell apart, you're back outside in the jungle with the crazies. Leave right now.

ADAM: This is not just about you and me, Jan.

JAN: *I* know that, Adam. Do you?

ADAM: What happens to Greg?

JAN: I'm with you on that one, honey. I just can't seem to give a shit.

ADAM: Don't you fucking dare—

JAN: Did you think if you were found out, the marriage would survive?

ADAM: I thought a million things, and none of them matter right now.

JAN: But when they mattered you must have considered the consequences and you didn't let that stop you.

ADAM: Jan, let's just forget what I did to you for a moment, and think about how to do what's best for Greg.

JAN: Too late. We already did the worst thing we could—we had him.

ADAM: I can't believe the shit that comes out of your mouth.

JAN: That's the bottom line, though. It's what you really think. He got strapped with a busy, cold, foul-tempered, withholding mom . . .

ADAM: You say such incredibly stupid things—

JAN: If you'd known I was like this, if you'd believed me when I said how much I didn't want to have a child, if you knew what kind of mother I'd turn out to be, would you have wanted me to have Greg?

ADAM *(Avoiding her eyes)*: Of course—

JAN: Look at me, Adam. This marriage is over. Do you understand that. It's okay to be completely honest with me. I hate motherhood. I knew I'd hate it. I knew I'd be bad at it. I hate how important it is to you, I hate that I took on something I wouldn't do well because I can't stand to do any job less than perfectly, that's how I'm made, and most of all I hate knowing, and I do know this, I've always known I did it because if I hadn't, I'd lose you. That was selfish. I had Greg for selfish reasons. When I see that poor little mouse watching me with those gray eyes, seeing through my attempts at affection, I know he knows . . . And then I hate you for making me bring a life into the world that has to grow up knowing his mother wishes he didn't exist.

ADAM: He knows nothing of the kind. And it's just not true.

JAN: If you knew then what you know now, would you have made such a big deal of having a child with me?

ADAM: You're an excellent mother.

JAN: Look at me, Adam. Answer my question.

ADAM (*Very difficult*): If you knew I'd fuck around, would you have married me?

JAN: Never in a million years.

ADAM: Well that's a lie, you see. Because you *did* know.

JAN: Believe me, if I'd known, we would not be here today.

ADAM: Every other Monday, home at three in the morning.

JAN: Book Circle. You were with those book readers.

ADAM: With the smell of fresh soap on me—I always showered at the office.

JAN (*In spite of herself*): And that horrible locker-room deodorant.

ADAM: You went rigid when I lay down.

JAN: I didn't "go anything," I was asleep.

ADAM: Is that how you remember the "horrible deodorant" . . .

JAN: I smelled it when we woke up.

ADAM: We were just learning how to hurt each other back then. We were amateurs.

JAN: I never once suspected you. I decided to trust you and I've stood by that decision ever since.

ADAM: It's no good, the martyred innocent crap. You could have busted me anytime, but then you'd have to stay with me *knowing what I was.* Your life wouldn't be unfair, it would be a choice you made with your eyes wide open, and there'd be no one to blame but yourself, and you *chose*, Janine . . . because you were twenty-eight, and lonely, and scared men off by your incredible glamour and lack of feminine tricks and, and because after years around male dancers you were scared of, what was that incredible thing you told to the borough president's wife, that fundraiser thing, "*I'm really not comfortable with men who want a part of their body inside mine* squirting." God, the look on her face, I'll never forget . . .

JAN: What's the point? The marriage is over. You're leaving.

ADAM *(Quieter)*: I'm not leaving. You kicked me out.

JAN: It's a formality. You were gone ten years ago.

ADAM *(Sincere)*: No. I thought about it. Yes, I did, I— And I thought about it again when I started this job . . . I thought I'd look her up, have dinner. If she was anything like remembered her, if she made me feel the way she did back then . . . desirable, accepted, important in her life . . .

JAN: You are such a disappointment.

ADAM: Well that's marriage: two people who disappoint each other, just not quite enough to go their own way.

JAN *(Stony)*: Good-bye.

(Adam approaches her quietly, slowly, trembling with suppressed rage. She calmly lifts her glass, sips, then sets it back down with delicate precision. Adam smashes his hand on the table with all his strength. Jan recoils.)

—You're *crazy*, Adam! Get out of my house.

ADAM: *Your* house?

JAN: Everything here belongs to me. Greg is mine. You can't have him. I'll take everything away from you.

ADAM *(Starts out)*: I'll see you in the morning.

JAN: Take your bag.

ADAM: I'm going to bed. Upstairs, in my house.

(She rises and starts for the phone.)

JAN: I'll call the police.
ADAM: When I hit you, I thought I could never do that again, but it's not true, I could hurt you so badly right now . . .
JAN: Go ahead. A bruise, and a cut on my foot. That'll pretty much settle the custody issue.

(She reaches for the phone.)

ADAM: You're going to call them?

(She puts her hand on the phone, a threat.)

I'll be upstairs.

(He goes upstairs.)

JAN *(Calling out)*: Adam!!! *(No answer) ADAM!!!!*

(She seems lost, and in a rage all at once. She wanders aimlessly. She takes the valise, walks around with it, then places it by the front door again.
   She looks toward upstairs, then goes to the phone. She almost lifts it, but doesn't.
   She wanders again, repeating the word: "No," over and over. Her tone runs from pleading, to rage, to command and, finally, to a disbelief that this can be happening.)

No. No, no, no. No, no, no, no, no NO NO NONONO!!!

(She is frozen in the middle of the room.
   Adam reenters, fully dressed.)

What are you doing?

ADAM: Calling a car. You're right. It's over.

JAN: And if she wasn't out there waiting for you, fucking coward?

ADAM *(Now he is calm)*: Tim offered to buy me out. He was calling I'm pretty sure to lower his price. And I've decided to accept. There's a teaching position at U-Penn, *tenure track*; they invited me to apply. The department has some of my models on display in the lobby—I had no idea. My work is actually still held in esteem here and there, imagine!

(He starts to dial, then stops, struck by a further thought.)

When we first fucked, me and Melinda—this time 'round I mean, not the early encounters—she asked me something, *"Does it feel nice what I'm doing right now?"* I misunderstood, I thought I'd failed to notice something and she needed praise, the way you, dear, need constant recognition for every inconsequential little thing you do during the day, and I give it, and you sneer and pretend you're insulted by the compliment, even though you're secretly pleased . . . But her question, it hit me after a moment . . . she was trying to please me. To make me happy. I forgot that women did that. I thought she was up to something at first, you know, playing me. No. She was just—it was her habit / pleasing a man was what she tried to do without thinking. This may sound pitiful, Jan, but the sad truth is being treated that way, being thought of as someone who deserved to be pleased . . . it's phenomenal. It feels / I felt like a man. She made me feel like a man. Manly. Male. God, you're right, it's wonderful to talk to a stranger, someone you'll never see again. Imagine discovering at my age that a woman can make you feel masculine. It's comical, really, how powerful that is. How happy it makes her to use her power. And how happy her using it makes me feel. As opposed to your power to make me feel like a piece of shit. So, thinking it over, the choice between giving a woman the power to make me feel like shit, or to make me feel like a man, I've decided to spend what's left of my good years on earth as a male. With Lindy. I was almost about to turn my back on her. I was about to go out there and tell her I couldn't run off the way we'd planned. —If this night had gone a different way . . . if you'd dug into your heart and found in your power to spend an hour or two simply being not thoroughly unpleasant . . . But instead—she and I are going to marry. It's what she wants, and I want.

(He starts to lose it but buries the wave of grief under icy, measured anger.)

She has friends in Pennsylvania. They'll find us a place. We'll move there, far away from both the lives we've been trying to escape for years, because. Because. Because I hate you. Because I fucking hate how you refuse to let yourself be loved the way I wanted to, the way I could if you'd only let me. Because you made me want to do that for you more than anything on earth, then refused to let me do it.

(He dials a local car service number from a list beside the phone. He waits while the phone rings.
Jan is paralyzed.)

(Into the phone) Yes . . . hello, could I have a car at . . . At . . .

(Jan storms out.
Adam hangs up.
After a moment the phone rings. Disoriented, he wonders if the car company traced his number via callback. He answers.)

Hello? Hi—it's Adam. Slow down, Mrs. Pelligrini, I can't follow . . . What? *(Beat)* Here? What would he be doing—? *[here]* Mrs. Pelligrini, where is Greg. *(Beat)* No, he's somewhere in your house, he'd never wander outside in a strange neighborhood. No, forget the police, do me a favor; this may sound strange, but could you check all your closets and see if your clothes are there, and if they're not, look for a pile in some corner . . . and then look under the pile. *(Beat)* It's just . . . something I'd like you to do, okay? I'll wait here—

(Jan enters, alert. She heard the phone ring.)

JAN *(Loud whisper)*: Who is it?

(Adam lowers the phone.)

ADAM: Greg's missing.

JAN: Missing where?

ADAM: Mrs. Pelligrini checked her kid's room to see that everything was okay—

JAN: Call the police, tell them to start a search.

ADAM: She's looking for him.

JAN: He's gone, that's what you said. That means she already looked and couldn't find him.

ADAM: She's looking again. He's somewhere in the house.

JAN: Can't you do *anything* right, give me the phone. *(She snatches it)* Hello, Mrs. Pelligrini, hello? Where is she, why doesn't she answer?!

ADAM: Because she's looking for him.

(She hangs up and starts to dial.)

Now what?

JAN: I want the police, I want a search.

ADAM *(Grabbing the phone)*: No.

JAN: Let go of the phone.

(He pulls it away and replaces the receiver.)

You're going to just stand here wasting time while he wanders around Staten Island all alone at four in the morning—

ADAM: He's not wandering around anywhere. He'd never go out of the house on his own.

JAN: How do you know that?

ADAM: He's my son. I know what he'd do.

JAN: Please, Adam, call the police.

ADAM: We're not going to create a panic until we know there's something to panic about. Meanwhile, we're going to wait until Mrs. Pelligrini calls us back to say if they found him.

JAN: I told you he wasn't ready for a sleepover. You let him go all the way to Staten Island.

ADAM *(Calm)*: Yes. And if something happens, it'll be my fault, if that makes you feel any better.

JAN: He's somewhere alone out there trying to find his way home from god knows where . . .

ADAM: STOP IT!

JAN *(With mounting hysteria)*: Adam . . . Jesus, Adam, what's the matter with you, don't you understand anything?

ADAM *(Sharply)*: What?

JAN: Hold me.

(She trembles. He is astonished and unprepared. He holds her. She breaks down in huge racking sobs.)

ADAM *(Stroking her back)*: It's okay. It's okay, Neen, everything is / nothing bad has happened to Roo, he's playing "Come Find Me." He loves when people have to look for him, you know that . . . he's in no danger—

(The phone rings. Jan picks it up immediately.)

JAN: Hello? *(Beat)* Oh, thank god. Where was he? *(Beat)* Oh.
(Beat) May I talk to him please? *(She cups the phone a
moment and speaks to Adam)* He was in a closet. Under
clothing. *(To Greg, now on the phone)* Sweetie . . . hi.
How are you feeling? *(Beat)* A nightmare? *(Beat)* Well,
you're okay now, right? *(Beat)* Home? Don't you think
you could lie down there, with the lights on, and wait
until morning when Mommy can come get you . . .

*(Adam gestures that he can get a car and pick him up. She
waves him away.)*

What was that, sweetie? *(Beat)* It's very very late, is the
thing. *(Beat)* All right, let me talk to Mrs. Pelligrini.
(Beat) Hello . . . I'm so sorry about this. I'll come out
right away. *(Beat)* That's very kind but I can't ask you to
drive all that way, it's no problem, I'll call a service and
be there in half an hour. *(Cupping the phone, to Adam)*
I'll drop you off at the airport. *(Back on the phone. Beat)*
No, no, please, I'd really feel better if . . . *(Beat)* Really?
(Beat) Well, if you're absolutely sure. *(Beat)* Yeah, kids
do have nightmares, I know. *(Beat)* Well, you're really
being wonderful about it, thank you. *(She hangs up)*

    Joey wants to ride with him. Oh my god, the hamster,
we can't ask her to—with a hamster . . . look at the mess
you caused!

ADAM: It didn't sound as if Mrs. Pelligrini was very upset.

JAN: She's just being nice.

ADAM: Greg had a nightmare. He hid under some clothes.
Now he wants to come home. It's not the end of the
world.

JAN: What does it take for something to get through to you?

ADAM: What does it take for you to have a sense of proportion.

JAN: Did you call a car service? Just before? Is someone on the way?

ADAM *(Beat)*: Only our son.

JAN: What are we going to do, Adam?

ADAM: Could we possibly just not know for a few hours? Could we survive till the morning without a plan. Do some work. Get your mind off it.

(Softening) Are you okay?

JAN: No.

ADAM: I'll wait outside for Greg. It's a nice night.

JAN: Just stay here. We don't need neighbors seeing you out on the stoop at this hour. Dressed like that.

ADAM *(Adamant)*: Who gives a shit what the neighbors see.

JAN: Greg'll worry something's wrong if you're out there half undressed.

ADAM: A safe assumption. No wonder he burrows. After tonight, there won't be enough clothes in the entire world to hide under.

(He goes out the front.
She sits down to her work, looks at it, picks up a page, tries to focus, gives up.
She rises and looks toward the front door.)

JAN *(Calls)*: Close the door, Adam. Would you please close the door.

(With a sigh, she sits back down at the table and tries to work. She leans back to watch the door. She returns to her paperwork. She can't concentrate. The lights begin to dim.
Scene change:
The lights grow more dim as Jan sits at her work. She can't focus. She drifts into a reverie. Time passes.
The clock reads: 4:16 A.M.
The lights grow brighter on:)

SCENE 5

Adam comes in from outside, rubbing circulation back into his arms; it's chilly out there. He and Jan exchange a look. Jan glances at her watch.

JAN: How long could it possibly take to drive from Staten Island?

ADAM: Forty minutes. With the hamster cage maybe a few hours.

(She gets eggs from the fridge, plus a block of cheddar cheese, while Adam starts to sweep broken glass into a dustbin.)

What's that for?

JAN: He'll be hungry when he gets home.

ADAM: At this hour?

JAN *(Her calm tone signals deep trouble)*: Him and his rituals: house, door, food—he needs routines. Cheese omelet. *(Beat)* And cinnamon toast. I'd like that recipe, please.

(She takes a grater from a drawer.)

ADAM *(Thinking it through)*: It's better I'm here when he gets home, don't you think? I shouldn't leave before he gets here. You and me are one thing but / Is the marriage over, Jan?

JAN: Even though you swept the floor, you mean? Does that make up for the other little awkwardness?

ADAM: I can't undo what I've done.

JAN: Then yes, I guess it's over.

ADAM: How do we tell Greg?

JAN: I thought we stopped planning for the rest of the night.

(He dumps the glass into the garbage.)

ADAM *(Beat)*: I'm done here. Would you like to come inspect? Offer criticism?

(Jan comes and looks.)

JAN: Very good job.

ADAM: You don't have to say that. Just because the marriage is over.

(She looks at her watch. She returns to grating the cheese.)

JAN *(Casually)*: At least we chose a lucky neighborhood. We'll get triple what we paid for the house.

ADAM: You're not / you can't sell—Gregory loves this place, you'd break his heart.

JAN: Everything'll break his heart now.

ADAM: Why make it worse?

JAN: Better a new start. He loves St. Augustine. Granny and Grandpa. All those cousins. The electric golf cart. Wild alligators.

ADAM *(Cornered; desperate)*: If you're trying to show me how it feels to be at the shit end of a deal, you've succeeded. And now . . . before we set out to destroy what's left of our son's world, I have to know / tell me if there's any way on earth—

JAN: What?

ADAM: Any way that we can—

JAN: We can *what?*

ADAM: Be together. I'll do anything you say, I'm quite serious.

JAN *(With quiet fury)*: You don't know what serious is. If you could see inside me now, you'd die from the pain. You took my power away.

ADAM: By sleeping with another woman? What's that got to do with power? Sex, okay. Desire, yes . . .

JAN: Things I don't arouse.

ADAM: Of course you do. But they're not important to you, they don't matter like other / Look, I understand the importance of work that *means* something, I didn't get as far as I have by doing my job carelessly or without devotion, but at the end of the day, when it's time for the reward, I can't wait to get home, to be with you, pour some wine, fix dinner, talk about our day and wait for things to get a little exciting, dangerous . . . that's what I live for, not the dishes, the bills, Greg's bath, sweeping the front stoop, the only things you seem to communicate with me about, the routines . . . we're living for routines. I want *you.*

JAN *(Beat)*: Oh, Adam, I could make all this unimportant. I could. The only problem's always been . . . I love you more than I ever knew it was possible to love anything on earth. If I just could somehow not know how lucky

I was to have found you . . . *(Sobbing hugely)* Oh, Adam, you motherfucking lowlife piece of shit, no man ever born is as beautiful to me as you are, no one knows me, understands me, loves me the way you have . . . *(He moves toward her)* —Stay away, don't you dare fucking try and make it better—

ADAM: Janine, you're scaring me—

JAN: I hope so. When the kind of love I feel turns bad, I'm that movie: "*Be afraid, be very afraid.*"

ADAM: Jan . . .

JAN: You want me back, return my power. Make my house safe again.

ADAM: I can't undo what I did.

JAN: Give me back what you took away. If it's important. If you really love me.

ADAM: I never stopped loving you. What I did took nothing away from that.

JAN: You put our life at risk. Isn't our safety a big thing to take away?

ADAM: If I told you I'd never do it again—

JAN: You can't know that. You can mean it in the moment, but a man as weak and needy as you, sentenced for life to an irritable bitch like me, how could I hold anyone to such a promise—

ADAM: Then what, what are you asking?

JAN: Tell me about her.

ADAM: Why?

JAN: Do you love me? You said you did. Does her husband know? About you, I mean?

ADAM: My god, no. He's running for public office. If it ever got out about me and his wife, their life would go up in smoke.

JAN: Would she care? Does she love him?

ADAM: Jan, let's not drag ourselves through this—

JAN: You talked to her about me, didn't you. Well?

ADAM: A little.

JAN: I'm claiming equal rights. How did you meet . . . oh, that reading club. How did you seduce her, the backseat of a taxi?

ADAM: Actually, it was outside an elevator.

JAN: Oh, my. Have we no imagination?

ADAM: Come to think of it, in the hallway with her—I pictured you.

JAN: Using your wife as a fantasy when you cheat. I have no idea what to feel about that.

ADAM: It's pretty fucking strange, for sure.

JAN: She had two children?

ADAM: Yes.

JAN: How old are they now?

ADAM: I don't know, late teens—

JAN: Are they fucked-up?

ADAM: Jan?! What are you doing.

JAN: Trying to picture her life. Is it good? Does she value what she has? Does she feel, I don't know, the way I always have about my life until tonight. Blessed.

ADAM: I didn't used to think so. But when we talk about running off together, she seems to drift . . . like she doesn't really want to go there. She's been careful to control our affair. We both have, actually. And I imagine the effort cost her a lot, she's pretty / she's a highly emotional woman.

JAN: So . . . if she knew I knew everything; if her husband found out—what would happen?

ADAM: I think / I guess it might be . . . pretty messy.

JAN: Good. Maybe there's light at the end of this tunnel after all.

(She brings paper and a pen to the table.)

Write down her phone number.

ADAM: Why?

JAN: Because you said you'd do anything to get me back. Because you can't make up for what you did, so I'll handle it.

ADAM: How?

JAN: I'll call and tell her husband about you and his wife.

ADAM: Jan, you can't.

JAN: Write down the number.

ADAM: What's the idea here?

JAN: To destroy their life.

ADAM *(Sudden terror, masked by utter calm)*: I see. And what would that accomplish?

JAN: I'm not trying to accomplish anything, this is about revenge—doing to her what she almost did to me.

ADAM: I get your point, I see what you're saying—

JAN: Then write.

ADAM: Jan, think about this—

JAN: Do you love me?

ADAM: You know I do.

JAN: How much? Not enough to protect our world, but maybe enough to ruin theirs? I'm serious, Adam, if you want me back, these are my terms; write her number.

ADAM: No.

JAN: Then leave.

(She brings him his valise.)

ADAM: Why will destroying someone else's life make things right?

JAN: Because it's exactly what I want to do. The way you wanted to fuck another woman, and did it. And how I wanted to dance, and didn't. And how you wanted your own firm, and did it. And I wanted to be special like everyone said I was, but . . . I had a baby instead. My excuse. My cop-out. I'm such a fucking coward. But

143

tonight, I want something. I want to destroy. And I won't be denied. Give me the number.

ADAM *(With an angry glint)*: You'd never dare. You're not that cruel.

(He writes down the number.)

JAN: There's a first time for everything. Do you plan to stay and listen?

ADAM *(Trying to take command)*: Greg'll be here any second. I have to be at the airport in three hours. Let's save this till I get back.

JAN: Let's not.

(She starts dialing.)

ADAM: Put down the phone. Jan, put it down.

JAN *(Cupping phone, offhand)*: What's her name, Melinda, did you say? "Melinda"! God, what does she do, spin wool and churn butter in the barn: "Melinda"!

ADAM: Just stop . . .

(He makes a move to press the cradle button on the phone. She blocks him.)

JAN *(Into the phone)*: Hi—

(Adam grabs the phone and they start to wrestle. Jan starts to assault him, flailing in a rage.)

I hate you, Adam. I want you dead. Go away from me and die.

(Finally they break apart. Jan speaks into the phone. Adam is spent, resigned to what's happening.)

Hello? This is Jan calling, Janine Penzius. I don't know if that name means anything to you, but my husband—my husband . . .

(She can't continue. She stands holding the receiver. Adam takes it and listens.)

ADAM: Hello? *(Beat)* Lindy?

(After listening a moment, he hangs up.)

JAN: He hung up?
ADAM: It was a man?
JAN *(Deflated)*: Why did I do that? God, how stupid.
ADAM: Maybe they'll think it's a wrong number.
JAN: Who cares about *them*. I behaved like a fool.

(The phone rings. They freeze, looking at each other.)

ADAM: They must have callback.
JAN: Maybe it's Greg. Answer the phone.

(He picks up, says nothing. Just listens. Then he hangs up.)

ADAM: Why, Jan, why did you have to start this?
JAN: I'm trying to finish what *you* started.

(Neither knows what to do now. She looks around the kitchen, starts to take something from the counter, stops. Then she moves to the table and begins straightening the tablecloth.)

I hate this tablecloth. The colors are so blech.

(Adam wanders a few steps. He stops.)

ADAM: What's the situation here? Where are we?

JAN: I'm not sure. I'm kind of playing it by ear.

(She straightens the tablecloth more carefully.)

Don't you have to say good-bye to her? You had plans to see her out there, didn't you say? You have my permission by the way. I think it's the right thing to do.

(Adam watches her.)

(Still upset about her behavior on the phone) Tell her I know everything, you can even tell her I threw a fit . . . you'll figure something out, you're pretty glib and convincing when you put your mind to it.

ADAM: Jan—

JAN: But you can't fuck her again. No, I don't want that. Actually, I forbid it.

ADAM: You're sick.

JAN: I'm your wife; that you want so much to not lose. *(Sensing how things finally stand)* And you gave me her number. Now the power's mine again . . . whenever I want. So, our marriage might not be over.

ADAM: Is that the next hurdle? Making yourself so scary I won't want you?

JAN: I thought we passed that one years ago! You betrayed me, I scared you—now we're onto the next test. What will it be I wonder? And will we pass that one? Stay tuned, folks.

(What they both yearn for now is Greg to be home, to escape into familiar rituals.)

We might survive the whole damn war, end up one of those old couples you see in restaurants staring into space, chewing, nothing left to say . . . all that silent history; the wounds, the love. One of those fifty words. Who knows, maybe we'll get there. Maybe not.

(She kisses his cheek. It's tender and strange at the same time. She goes to the fridge, takes some things out, glances at her watch.)

What are they, *crawling* from Staten Island?

ADAM *(Watching her warily)*: Jan, I need some clarity here. We have to decide what we'll tell Greg. We can't go on fighting each other *through* him, it's too confusing.

(Adam waits for a response. None comes.)

Do you truly accept me after what I did? Can we stop being angry? Can we meet each other halfway here—without Greg between us? Without making him afraid?

(She looks at him. Beat.)

Please say something. Jan?

(He waits.
Doorbell. They look toward the front door.)

JAN: He's home.

(Adam is unsure what to do.)

Go out and help with the hamster cage.

(He starts out. As he passes her, she grasps his hand impulsively—an acknowledgment. For a moment they stay like this, hand in hand, not looking at each other.
Then he goes out.
After a moment she calls out:)

Tell him I'm making an omelet.

(No answer. Calling again:)

(Needing to keep a connection) And check he has his backpack.

(She starts cracking eggs for the omelet. Life resumes.
    The lights begin to slowly fade.
    She looks toward the front door.
    She stirs the eggs.
    She looks toward the door again.
    The lights continue to fade, then—
    Blackout.)

END OF PLAY

SIDE EFFECTS

PRODUCTION HISTORY

Side Effects received its world premiere on June 19, 2011, by MCC Theater (Robert LuPone, Bernard Telsey and William Cantler, Artistic Directors; Blake West, Executive Director) at the Lucille Lortel Theatre in New York. It was directed by David Auburn; the scenic design was by Beowulf Boritt, the costume design was by Wade Laboissonniere, the lighting design was by Jeff Croiter, the sound design was by Scott Killian; the production stage manager was Kelly Glasow. The cast was:

LINDY	Joely Richardson
HUGH	Cotter Smith

SCENE 1

A dark living room, late at night. The beige curtains are drawn. If open, we'd see a winter street in a stately suburban neighborhood of a small Midwestern metropolis.

Lindy (Melinda) Metz sits motionless on a sofa. An outside light penetrates the curtains, outlining Lindy's head and shoulders from behind.

A cloud of smoke rises from her cigarette. She holds a tumbler in her lap which has only a few pebbles of ice left at the bottom. Her winter coat is flung over the sofa back.

She raises her cigarette, inhales deeply. A long pause. She expels a jet of smoke.

Headlights swing past outside. The noise of a car engine grows louder, then stops. The headlights go out. The room is dark again. Utter quiet.

Lindy cocks her head almost imperceptibly, listening. A car door opens and shuts. Footsteps crunch on a snowy driveway. The sounds are crisp and vivid, as if heard by a too-sensitive ear.

*A key jiggles in the lock. The door opens. Hugh peers
into the darkness. He unbuttons his overcoat. We see that he is
dressed for a dinner party.*

He locates Lindy in the dark.

HUGH: You're here. *(No response)* Lindy?

LINDY: Lindy's here.

*(Hugh stamps snow off his shoes, advances inside. He is
a vigorous man with a small mustache; an outdoor type:
hunter, golfer, skier; a man the public would trust.*

*He is upset, but in total control of what he allows people
to see.)*

HUGH: Sitting in the dark.

LINDY: So it would appear. To those who can see me.

HUGH: Why aren't you asleep?

LINDY *(Beat)*: How do you know I'm not? *(Beat)* Come to that,
how do *I* know?

HUGH: Close your eyes I'm turning on the light.

LINDY: Just *leave* it, Hugh, please—

*(He turns on the lights. Lindy is dressed for a dinner party,
perhaps more flair than necessary, but subtle. Her features
are striking, sensual, and she needs little makeup.*

*The room is done in neutral, calming colors. Trophies
and photos of vintage bicycles line the room, plus a garish
LeRoy Neiman–style print of a Tour de France cyclist
crossing the finish line.*

*The rest of the large house exists off, kitchen, den, stairs
to the second floor, etc.)*

HUGH: Are you going to sit here and wallow?

LINDY: This isn't a wallow. It's a "me-feeling-peaceful." Feeling the way I'd choose to feel, even if I had a choice.

HUGH *(Comes closer; opting for civility)*: I made excuses.

LINDY: *Did* you?!

HUGH: Flu.

LINDY: That was enough to satisfy the *(Parody)* Schtubbin-Schmubbins?

HUGH: Steubenhauers. *(Pronounced "Stoy-bin-our")*

LINDY: Yes, Hugh, I know their name. I was being funny, remember when we were funny, when we laughed a lot?

HUGH: Do you have any idea how embarrassing / Those are longtime family friends, important people in this city. And Mother sitting right there; it's bad enough at the best of times with you two— *(Rallies)* Mother sent Isador home with the sedan and made me drive her all the way back to Oakville alone so she could chew my ear off—

LINDY *(Imitating the imperious Mama Metz)*: "That woman has been nothing but trouble from day one. Why you had to go and marry a complete outsider—"

HUGH: Close enough.

LINDY: I've only had half a century to get on her good side. They say that's the tricky stretch.

HUGH: I told them you've been fighting that bug that's going 'round, in case anyone asks. I tried to talk you into not coming tonight, but you were so eager to know them better . . .

(He sits and removes his rubbers.)

LINDY: Yes, I couldn't wait to be put on display, laid out on a microscope slide for inspection . . .

HUGH: . . . To just up and vanish like that in the middle of the main course, not a word to anyone; I call that extremely poor choice-making.

LINDY *(With relish)*: Did you use those words? "I apologize for my wife's sudden departure. It was extremely poor choice-making on her part"?

(Hugh chuckles despite himself. She stands. She turns down the light.)

HUGH: Why, Lindy?

LINDY: And what did the Smug and Mighty of our great mini-metropolis have to say about my piss-poor choice-making?

HUGH: Nothing. I explained; they listened. I'm sure tongues will wag.

LINDY: "I apologize?"

(She sits again. Hugh puts his rubbers neatly by the door.)

HUGH: Where's my umbrella?

LINDY: I told you I was bringing it in for repairs.

HUGH: No, Lindy, you did not tell me, because if you had told me I would have stopped you.

LINDY: It was falling apart.

HUGH: That umbrella doesn't leave this house—it's a museum piece—

LINDY: There's a dozen more just like it under reverential glass in the factory lobby, alongside the failed sewing machine and the failed baby buggy—Grandpa Gustav's Hall of Failures, the great warm-up for, ta-da: *(Finger quotes)* "The Metz Bicycle." Why on earth was he so eager to show off his fuck-ups? Don't normal people try and hide things like that?

HUGH: He's celebrating perseverance. Grandpa Gustav never gave up.

LINDY: Ugh-oh, your *lecture* tone. I'm being told something, something indirect about—what?—about *leaving the dinner party?* Yes, I failed to persevere. I fled. Now I'm wallowing. Got it.

(Hugh turns the light up again. He studies her.)

HUGH *(Beat)*: Are you going to explain?

LINDY: Is the "umbrella conversation" officially closed?

HUGH: What happened back there?

LINDY: Didn't you get my message?

HUGH: I got your text.

LINDY *(So there)*: Well then.

HUGH: "I'm going home."

LINDY: And home I went. And down I sat. And here you found me. You've missed not a single episode in my exciting life and times.

HUGH: Is this your adolescent way of telling everyone you don't need their approval?

LINDY: Hugh, for pity sake, you heard their conversation, they were calling *abortion* a sin against God.

HUGH: It's noise, meaningless cocktail jibber-jabber.

LINDY: It was an attack on me— They all read the editorial page.

HUGH *(Puzzled)*: Your letter didn't mention abortion.

LINDY: It's code, Hugh. I was inviting all those well-padded fräuleins to visit my class at Coolidge Vocational and meet some of the Special Ed kids they're all so eager to help be born—Keeshon, for example, who I didn't mention by name—seventeen years old and looks twelve from malnourishment, and he stutters, too, ever since his crack-ho mom was shot to death when he was nine, and he had to bring up his twin baby sisters alone because he was the only male left in the family, with no free clinic to treat him when he got HIV from pimping his butt on the street to pay for food. While he completed ninth grade with severe memory and speech impairment. If they're so eager to keep Keeshon's mother from sinning against God by sparing him his unspeakably cruel existence, they might sacrifice some of that farm-raised venison and baby asparagus they were stuffing into their face-holes and use the money to support schools and clinics . . . They knew

exactly who my letter attacked and they were sticking it
to me—

HUGH: And by walking out you gained what?

LINDY: Nothing. I gained . . . *(Stops)* Good point.

HUGH: What aren't you telling me?

LINDY: What aren't you telling *me?*

HUGH: You've sat through much worse. Why take offense at a
bunch of cackling hens.

LINDY: Well, shouldn't someone take offense? Shouldn't you?

HUGH: None of them are in your league, they'd kill for a tenth
your style. You can keep a room spellbound—when you
try . . .

LINDY: I thought my poetic flights annoyed you.

HUGH: Lindy, you intimidate them . . . starting a new
career—a graduate degree at your time of life . . . and
your incredible success with these kids, it's not what they
know . . .

(She stands, again turns down the light.)

LINDY: So why drag me onto the scales for them to weigh?

HUGH: One night—is that too much to ask?

LINDY: You're running for City Council, it's a nothing
office. —Sorry, that came out wrong, but that's pretty
much how you put it to me, with the understanding that
at this level a wife can side-step the political circus—

HUGH: Tonight was a courtesy. They want to feel comfortable
with us . . . as a couple.

LINDY *(Holding out her glass)*: A wee splash?

HUGH: That's not a great idea right now.

LINDY: I'm not competing for a Great Ideas Award, I just want
a fucking drink thank you. *(Genuinely apologetic)* Sorry. A
"gosh-darned" drink. *(Moving toward the bar)* Never mind.

HUGH *(Stopping her with a gesture)*: Give me the glass. *(He
takes it from her, and moves to make them drinks)*

LINDY: Halfway to the top. No water. No ice.

(*Dull thumps from upstairs. Hugh glances at the ceiling.*)

HUGH: Is that Doug?

LINDY (*With a fond smile*): Unless we have a heavy metal polterghost. Geist. Is "geist" plural of ghost?

HUGH: He should be in bed.

LINDY: Doug is sixteen. When he's ready for bed, he'll manage it all by himself.

HUGH: While the boys live at home, they'll keep civilized hours.

LINDY: At Doug's age I was sleeping in bus stations. We grow up when we have to.

HUGH: I don't understand . . . Wilson, like clockwork, ten P.M. out like a light, never a problem, but Doug—how could two brothers be less alike . . .

LINDY: The law of proportion? One normal child for the healthy parent; and a Mystery-Boy for the Queen of the Moon.

HUGH: Stop it, Lindy. You know how I hate that kind of talk. You're so much better than this, if you'd just— (*He stops himself*)

LINDY (*Finishing for him*): If I'd just take my meds? Yes, all right. I apologize. I tried this time, really I did. The new cocktail makes my hands tremble. If I have to choose between suffering through a dinner party with too much mood *sans* pills, or flipping venison off the tip of my fork because my current miracle mix makes me vibrate like a jackhammer, I'll take my chance with moodiness. And when talk turned to the sins of the Pregnant and Desperate, my old Lindy-Beast awoke, you know how I get—so I decamped . . . discreetly, I thought. I even folded my napkin into an adorable little tepee, just like Mrs. Steubenhauer set it, did you notice? . . .

HUGH: Did Doug come in while—

LINDY: Did he see Weird Mom sitting alone in the dark—in formal attire?

HUGH: I'm asking a simple question, Melinda. Please answer me.

LINDY: "Melinda"! Ugh-oh. Whole name, bad sign.

HUGH: Did he—

LINDY: —Yes, Hugh. He came in, he noted his mother's festive attire. He asked if I had a good time. I told him I had, and—what? I asked how was his night, he said *nothing special*, and I said *I know what you mean, Dougie-Bug*, then— I think that covers it.

HUGH: Did you have any . . . further exchange with him?

LINDY: Are you watching some new legal show? "Did there come a time when you had a further exchange with your son?"

HUGH: This is exactly what / Can you see why I'm worried— this is what happens every time, not just the random behavior, it's the whole *thing*, the compulsive chatter, the *performance*—for who, what pretend-audience is out there adoring every little twist of your mind, because the only one I see here is me.

LINDY (*Looking at him for a moment*): Yes. There's only you.

HUGH (*Watching her, not sure how far he wants to take this*): Are you really all right?

LINDY: Come here, baby. Come to Lindy-Witch. Sit, sit, rest your weary soul beside my still waters.

(*She pats the sofa, inviting a lapdog. Hugh sets down his drink.*)

HUGH: Are the pills in your vanity?

LINDY: Can't it wait till morning.

HUGH (*On his way to get her pills*): We'll look into new medication next week. I'll call Dr. Vine. Meanwhile— let's err on the side of caution.

(He almost turns up the light, hesitates, then exits.
Lindy thinks. She takes out her cell phone. She starts to
dial, then stops.
Hugh reenters with water and her pills.)

LINDY *(Regarding her phone, a blithe cover-up)*: No messages!
But behold: "husband bearing pills." Looks like the best
offer going.
HUGH *(Handing her the pills)*: Two yellow, one blue.
LINDY: Half the Special Ed kids I teach are on meds. How
did the world manage before we learned to correct God's
little boo-boos? *(Taking the pills from him)*
HUGH *(Sitting)*: Is there something more going on here, Lindy.
I know when you're slipping. Tonight felt—different.
LINDY: If I tell you exactly what happened . . . will you make
love to me?
HUGH *(Tense)*: Take your pills.
LINDY: Once they kick in, I won't be my whole self. Not much
time left to play with your Natural Woman. *(Swallowing
a pill)* Look, she's disappearing. *(Sings to herself, a cheer-
ful children's ditty:)*

The yellow ones make her normal
The blue ones make her calm
The green ones bring her happy thoughts . . .
She's going, going—*goooone*!!!

(She sips some water.)

HUGH: There's two more.
LINDY: Stop being such a pill nazi. Let me swallow this one
first.
HUGH *(Taking her drink)*: I'll put that on the sideboard—
LINDY: Don't touch.
HUGH: You're not supposed to mix pills with—

LINDY: What would we do without the things we're not supposed to do. *(Catching herself)* Whoops, random broadcast, sorry!

HUGH: Lindy, try to control yourself.

LINDY: Has it ever occurred to you that even when I'm wobbling a little on my axis, what I say is still valid, even insightful?

HUGH *(Knowing better than to engage this; clipped)*: We'll talk in the morning.

LINDY *(With feeling)*: Please, don't go all cold and withdrawn. I know, I *know*; and the part of me you want to escape is the same part I wish *I* could. If you'd just try a little harder not to remind me of it 24-7.

HUGH *(Yielding a little)*: I never know what to expect.

LINDY: Welcome to the club.

HUGH *(Beat)*: They were really upset. *(Sharing the postmortem)* Mrs. Steubenhauer didn't say a word when I left. Not even a: "Call when she's feeling better."

LINDY: Hildy Steubenhauer's social graces failed her?! Question: What remains when you subtract etiquette from Hildegard Steubenhauer? Answer: Seven yards of silk around four tons of lard.

HUGH *(A bark of laughter)*: Lindy! *(He wants to keep this serious but finds her amusement irresistible)*

LINDY: She *is big*, honey-bun. Well, more *immense* . . . monumental, yes! If something her size fell to earth the impact would raise clouds of dust; she'd cause a new ice age. Whole species would perish.

HUGH *(Chuckling)*: Hildy enjoys her food, she can't help herself.

LINDY *(Snapping)*: I can't help being bipolar.

(Sudden tension again.)

HUGH *(With great tact)*: Don't we all want the same / it's been a very stressful time; your certification was huge, the exam alone, and running your first classroom. You earned every bit of it, and the last thing we want is a setback.

LINDY: Yes, I'm a minefield, the least wrong step . . .

HUGH: That's not what I mean. It's triggers. I didn't see one tonight. And if something just takes hold, and we miss the signs . . . you don't want to end up stapling the curtains shut and hiding under the sink again . . .

LINDY: Stop, Hugh, stop making me the villain here when it's you who—when the whole thing is—

HUGH *(Genuinely puzzled; tense)*: Lindy, take a deep breath—

LINDY: Our gigantic hostess told me everything.

HUGH: About what?

LINDY: You asked Steubenhauer about *St. Andrew's Academy*. You're going to send my little Dougie-Bug away to boarding school—

HUGH *(Disgusted)*: Your "little Dougie-Bug" is sixteen years old, for pity sake—

LINDY: But St. Andrew's—chapel and blue blazers?! With his nipple rings and goth tattoos? What on earth are you thinking?!

HUGH: St. Andrew's instills discipline.

LINDY: Oh yes, and how good it sounds in the campaign literature: ". . . Son Douglas at St. Andrew's." You're worried he'll embarrass you with his late-night forays to god knows where to do god knows what with god knows who. We can't have any more of that with you running for—what, Hugh, what office was it again, it's not City Council anymore is it? . . .

HUGH *(Realizing she's learned the truth)*: I see.

LINDY: So it's true. Congress? Wow. Trent Collyer really has to step down? The child porn wasn't just a rumor.

HUGH: "Health issues" is the official line.

LINDY: And you're running in his place?

HUGH: Steubenhauer asked me. He's in a corner. I agreed to give it some thought. I already filed paperwork, the deadline's next week . . . but this only happens if you agree.

LINDY: Agree to sacrifice my privacy on the alter of public opinion?

HUGH: Let's not have this conversation till the pills take effect.

(She takes a pill.)

LINDY: United States Congress . . . that's a whole 'nother ball of wax, isn't it. I'd have to take the ride with you.

HUGH *(Trying to close the topic)*: In the morning, all right?

LINDY: Is Doug going away? Just tell me. Do I participate in this decision, or is it another edict from the Metz Dynastic Control Committee?

HUGH *(Patiently, slightly condescending)*: I asked Lute to see if a school like that is even an option with his grades. If it ever comes to a point where Doug needs more / a more *structured environment*, then Lute can call on his connections at St. Andrew's—

LINDY: Don't send Doug away. He needs me.

HUGH *(Calm)*: You indulge him. You make yourself responsible for his—

LINDY: Condition?

HUGH *(Agitated)*: There's no *condition*, Doug's just—you spend too much time with him shopping and meeting for lunch—he's picking up your moodiness, your sharp tongue . . . it's not genetic, it's far too soon to know a thing like that.

LINDY: Don't twist this around. You and Steubenhauer plan to exile our problem-child to some preppy gulag, don't you? Hugh, please answer me.

HUGH *(Irritated)*: There's one more pill.

(A moment goes by. Lindy is on a different track.)

LINDY: You may be in Steubenhauer's pocket, but I am not . . . and my children are not . . .

HUGH: In this town no Metz is in anyone's pocket. What Lute Steubenhauer wants, and what I want—we're useful to each other right now. He needs my name. And I need his influence.

LINDY: Is the company going under?

HUGH: Dear god, no, who said anything about . . . the plant's always up and down, it's cyclical. Cycles. *(Then)* A loan came due. The bank wouldn't restructure. I approached Steubenhauer. He fixed it.

LINDY: Just like that! *(Finger snap)*

HUGH *(With a slight swagger; despite himself)*: Two phone calls.

LINDY: So now you're *completely* in his pocket?

HUGH *(Growing increasingly flustered)*: No, Lindy . . . he needs someone he can trust, with no political baggage . . . and I need to keep the factory going if we want to enjoy—if we—if you'd make the *smallest effort* to understand this town . . . there's an unspoken agreement among the . . . the more established families . . . we stick together . . . Quaint, isn't it, worrying about my workers' employment. Grandpa Gustav's bicycles helped put this city on the map. Steubenhauer keeps the city afloat. I'm aware that considerations like that seem lowbrow to, you know, spiritually higher-up types like you— *(Exasperated)* I don't get it, I just / I've introduced you to just about everyone in this town, my friends, family friends, Lute's gang, and you hold yourself apart, like you're better than anyone because—why, why Lindy, what did you do that was so special, except hitchhike around Asia blissing out on drugs—

LINDY: We both did

HUGH: Yes, it was fun, but I came home, found work— What's so funny?

LINDY: I just had a flash of you standing outside that ashram in your Land's End hiking shorts—

HUGH: Don't change the subject—

LINDY: —wondering if you needed membership ID before they'd let you in.

HUGH: You know that's not what—I didn't know if they'd allow photographs inside. *(Realizes she's teasing him)*

LINDY: You're adorable when you stop trying to be someone.

HUGH *(At his wit's end)*: People here have done nothing but extend a welcome to you from the moment we moved back.

LINDY: *You* they welcomed, not *me*, not the exotic riffraff you dragged home. I remind them of the bad boy you were: "Mad Metz," who drank and drove motorcycles into the quarry—oh, and hung a swastika over the factory entrance and called his dad a union-busting nazi, then turned his back on this town and ran. Never mind that the prodigal son finally returned, tame and married, with two kids . . . I'm an outsider, I remind them you once made a whole life without them. And they're afraid they could lose you all over again to—oh, no!— *(Chuckles)* The Loony!

HUGH *(Doesn't know how to follow that)*: Promise me you'll apologize to Luther and Hildy. Call, drop by—you felt ill and didn't want to embarrass anyone . . .

LINDY: You're really going to run, aren't you. Congress. Christ.

HUGH: Lute says I'm a natural. But . . . I'm starting late in politics. I'll have to go all-out to make it happen. *(With meaning)* And I'll need your support.

LINDY *(Simply)*: Play with me.

HUGH *(Focusing)*: Promise you'll apologize. Flu. Something. It's not much to ask.

LINDY *(Looking at him long and hard)*: How much Lindy must I sacrifice to your ambitions?

HUGH *(Making a deeper defense)*: As much as I have for this family. It's time you met me halfway.

LINDY: Hugh?

HUGH: What?

LINDY: May I ask one favor?

HUGH *(Immediately solicitous)*: Of course.

LINDY: Until the pills kick in I can still climax.

HUGH *(Fighting to control his rage and panic)*: You sabotage an event that could have opened doors for me, and you expect to end the evening having your needs met . . .

LINDY: I withdraw the request.

(She takes a pill.)

HUGH: Think about that, Lindy. Think about the kind of woman who behaves that way.

LINDY: Some of us world-wanderers need love more than twice a year. Even after we've misbehaved, maybe *especially* then, 'cause maybe we're stirring the pot on purpose, to get your attention. You loved your Smutty-Witch once upon a time, when we'd run anywhere to relieve the itch: bathrooms, behind bushes, unlocked cars . . . even in the rain once, remember Birmingham, the statue of Vulcan, under your raincoat, all those people watching from the Public TV offices, *"Oh-no-they're-not-doing-what-I-think-they're-doing!"* God, wasn't that a hoot. You're aroused, Hugh, look! *(Referring to his crotch)* I can still make Puppy do tricks.

HUGH: We'll talk when the pills take effect.

LINDY: Let me finish you off, Hugh. Don't sneak to the bathroom after you think I'm asleep to pleasure yourself alone.

HUGH *(Withering)*: Nothing the pills can do to you is worse than this. *(He starts to leave)*

LINDY *(As if she's just remembered a detail)*: Oh, darling?

HUGH *(Turning sharply)*: What?

LINDY: Thank you for the understanding. Imagine if you had to fill yourself with drugs to serve *my* career—

(He leaves. Lindy moves to the bar. She puts her empty glass down. She starts to make another drink, but stops. She goes to her cell phone, stares at it. She checks the hall, making sure she is alone. Then she pushes the redial button. She waits. The lights dim, settling her into semi-darkness. Someone on the other end answers.)

(Startled) Adam?

(It's a message. Disappointed, she lowers the phone, then takes a deep breath and:)

Hello machine. I've been debating whether to return . . . *(Then)* Your message . . . I couldn't believe . . . ten years, Adam, how'd you track me down after all that time? *(Beat)* I snuck home tonight to be alone with your voice. *(She holds the phone away, talking to herself)* Shut up, Lindy. *(Into the phone)* Why were you in touch, why *now*?! *(Beat)* Strike the question. Please don't call again, Adam. *(Beat)* How is it you always stumble into my life when I'm wide open. *(To herself, sort of)* I didn't say that . . . *(Lowering the phone abstractly)* I'm sorry I vanished without— *(Beat)* I had to forget our time together—you, New York . . . poetry. All that. *(Into the phone)* Please don't call again.

(She hangs up.)

(Then, to herself) Stupid cow. Stupid, smutty, pathetic—
"*Moooo!*"

(She sits in the dim light, a smile on her face, as the lights fade.)

SCENE 2

Spring flowers (hyacinth and jonquil), in vases make vivid bursts of color around the room. Two suitcases (one large, one small red vanity) stand by the front door, which is slightly open.

Hugh enters from outside. He wears a T-shirt with his company logo and slogan—"Metz Bicycles: The Original, The Best." He is signaling to a driver outside.

HUGH *(Calling upstairs)*: Melinda, the car's waiting, get a move on.

LINDY *(From off)*: Is my raspberry vanity down there?

HUGH: I'll bring it to the car.

LINDY *(From off)*: No! I thought my lipstick was on the dresser, it must be in the vanity.

(Lindy comes downstairs in a traveling suit. She's breezy, relaxed, her hair stylishly short, she looks ten years younger.)

I asked you to take down the *big* suitcase, I can carry the little one—never mind, I'll repack at the airport.

HUGH: The driver's getting nervous. *(Looking at his watch)* You should allow forty-five minutes during rush hour.

LINDY: Where's Wilson?

HUGH: Football practice.

LINDY: That rat, he never wished me luck. *(Checking for something in her handbag)* I'll call him on the way to the airport . . . Wait, damn, his cell phone broke, third one this year. Oh, and there's a weekend of precooked meals in the freezer labeled by the day, and there's microwave instructions on post-its.

HUGH *(Stops her)*: Lindy?

LINDY: I'm excited, can you blame me? No, I'm—*aglow*.

HUGH: You've given speeches before, you'll be great.

LINDY *(Slyly)*: That's not what I mean Mister *Man*-man.

HUGH: Oh.

LINDY: Last night was spectacular. The new meds, honestly, toots, they're next door to heaven. *(Holds out her hands)* No trembles. *(Pats her tummy)* No weight gain. The big one on demand, side effects zero, just like a regular human being; if I'd known life could feel this good I'd have tried to grow up normal. Do you like my hair this way?

HUGH: You've asked me three times . . . *(Admiring her)* It's lovely. You're always . . . You're the most beautiful woman alive, Lindy. Well, it's true.

(Lindy glances in her compact mirror, fixing this and that, and discovering an amazing thing:)

LINDY: My god, you're right! Lucky you! Lucky me!

HUGH: Come on, Smutty-Witch, the car's waiting.

LINDY: Will you listen to my speech one more time.

HUGH: It's perfect, everything'll go like clockwork.

LINDY: The conference is *international*, for pity sake: Brazil, Cameroon, Japan, Hong Kong—you should see the list! Joachim Ben-Levi's *introducing me*—Ben-Levi wrote the standard text on developmental cognition! I'm a complete no one, I'm actually sort of a joke actually.

HUGH *(Steering her)*: Go. *(Mock bossy)* Now.

LINDY: I *hate* travel. All that time between places when no one knows where you are. You could wander off the edge of the world and be lost forever.

HUGH *(A little worried)*: Lindy?

LINDY: Whoops, morbid thoughts. Rewind: "Me—happy again." Oh, Hugh, come with me, we could have *fun* . . .

HUGH *(Considering)*: Hey, Miss Witch . . . focus. This weekend is about *you*. It's about *your* work, *your* achievements, *your* contribution.

LINDY: It's not like I was picked out of the wide world of Special Ed because of my, what, game-changing *master's thesis?*

HUGH: "Married Women with Second Careers," that's the demographic; you're a perfect fit.

LINDY: Oh dear, we have a disconnect. I'm going to a conference. *People* magazine's an add-on. Didn't Steubenhauer set it up?

HUGH: Steubenhauer doesn't tell *People* magazine who to feature. *(Beat, then)* It's possible his office was in contact with media people, I don't follow all that.

LINDY: Hugh, please. You're vulnerable in education. An article about your wife's results with her Special Ed kids could mean votes. Why else would I be asked to headline? Wasn't a large donation made to the conference, and didn't a certain airline whose CEO is Lute's brother-in-law arrange international travel for several dozen foreign luminaries in the field? Isn't *People* magazine to help position you nationally?

HUGH *(Carefully)*: Luther's staff supplies information to news outlets, it's standard procedure. If my wife happens to be

173

speaking at a conference, and *People* magazine gets wind of it, and *they* smell a good story . . .

LINDY: You really think I'd agree to weekends like this if it didn't help your campaign?

HUGH: I thought you disapproved of my decision to run. You really don't mind helping the campaign.

LINDY *(Gently)*: You deserve to be happy. Did I not apologize for the dinner party? I even endured Luther's tuna-salad-sandwich-and-bourbon-for-lunch breath while he groped me by his indoor swimming pool. How much lower do I have to stoop to pledge allegiance?

(She smiles a winning public grin. An understanding.)

HUGH: For *People* magazine, the main thing is—*stay on topic.* Education's all you discuss. For example, mention St. Andrew's, how much the boys enjoy it—

LINDY: Five C's, three D's and an F?

HUGH: I didn't say they're "doing well." They *enjoy it.*

LINDY *(Another public grin)*: Ah. Politics: "selective truth."

HUGH *(Overly casual)*: Oh, and the woman meeting you at the arrival gate is Lena Toller. Thirty-ish, she looks younger, short black hair, athletic build.

LINDY: *Lena Toller?*

HUGH: It's in your conference folder.

LINDY: And she's *who* again?

HUGH: An intern. Your assistant.

LINDY *(Beat)*: Why do I need an assistant?

HUGH: Look, she'll help with transportation, schedules, busy work. She has excellent taste—knows all the with-it night spots . . .

LINDY: "With-it night spots"?

HUGH: She's fun, everyone on the campaign loves her.

LINDY *(Finally getting it)*: So the guy at the last conference . . . with the oatmeal cardigan and brown loafers, he's history? I have a new tail, an actual pretend-intern. I wasn't sure about the loafer guy, I thought I was being paranoid, who'd want to follow *me*.

HUGH *(Beat. Full of warning)*: Steubenhauer's counting on me. After the near scandal with Trent Collyer, any hint of irregularity is a red flag.

LINDY: Why am I being watched?

HUGH: We're both recognized figures, Lindy. Your talk last month . . . Columbus—

LINDY: What about it?

HUGH: If information about visitors to your hotel room reached the wrong people . . .

LINDY *(No point denying it)*: Did you approve this?

HUGH: Lute's worried—that dinner party. He thought—

LINDY: "Loose cannon"?

HUGH: I never suspected—no one did.

LINDY: Suspected I had a friend?

HUGH: Is that what he is?

LINDY: Has anyone . . . contacted him?

HUGH: Adam Penzius?

LINDY: Oh god. What *else* do you know?

HUGH: He lives in New York. A son almost ten. Happily married. Architect.

LINDY: This is so sordid and cheap and—how *could* you?

HUGH: How could *I*? You had a man in your hotel room—

LINDY: For dinner. In my room because anywhere else someone might recognize me, I was trying to be discreet.

HUGH: Why didn't you tell me?

LINDY: Like you told me about getting Doug into St. Andrew's? I knew what you'd think. We have to be careful until you're in office, yes, but meanwhile I have no life, and it gets . . . lonely. What'll Steubenhauer do?

HUGH: He's letting us work it out.

LINDY: Meaning?

HUGH *(Covering his hurt)*: Who is this man?

LINDY: An acquaintance. From New York days. Someone to talk to. Someone . . . different.

HUGH: Did you sleep with him?

LINDY: I won't have this conversation. I can forgive Steubenhauer's horrible hands-down-my-panties "accidentally-on-purpose." I'll even squint at the things he does do to win votes, including this ridiculous "Married Women with Second Careers" interview for *People* fucking magazine, but I will not give up my privacy.

HUGH: If all you do is talk, is it worth the risk? You can find people here to talk to . . . we have some interesting friends.

LINDY: It's not the same. *(Beat. Then deciding to level with him)* He's— All right we met in a book club. / The boys were little / before your father died . . . back in New York, when we were still living *our way* / when we thought we escaped our past. —My god, how heroic you seemed to me; fearless. I had an amazing life—poetry, two sweet little boys, you were making noise on Wall Street. Adam's friends, they were—I don't know, another universe, opinionated, passionate, intense . . . whereas you . . . I don't mean things weren't good, my god our life was a fairy tale, and I saw how proud you were to show me off . . . your prize. But the flaw we ignored when it was just the two of us living wild . . . once the children were born, there was no avoiding it . . . And you—withdrew.

HUGH: Did you sleep with him?

LINDY: I'll say this once, then you tell Steubenhauer to back off.

HUGH: You're in no position to make ultimatums—

LINDY: Doug's away. Willy wants to join him at St. Andrew's. No one's left in our house except me and my enormous Bicycle King, who takes up all the air in our universe. It's *your* world, Hugh. Mine is teaching. And Adam. Those are mine.

HUGH (*With heartbreaking simplicity*): Do you love me, Melinda?

LINDY (*Blindsided*): What?

HUGH: You've seen everything I am. I need . . . I need—

(*Startled and thrown by his show of feeling, she holds him. The sudden tenderness shatters his customary control, and one enormous sob escapes.*)

LINDY: Poor baby. No more politics. Your heart's too honest. Don't give yourself away.

(*He pulls away gently, then stills himself.*)

HUGH: Sorry. Little emotional moment there. I'm good again.

LINDY (*Gentle, but emphatic*): Our private life is off-limits. Tell Steubenhauer.

HUGH: Not an option. You'll have to stop seeing this man.

LINDY: Or?

HUGH: I'd have to quit the campaign. And that's . . . problematic.

LINDY: "Problematic."

HUGH: Please take this to heart, Lindy.

LINDY: Tell Steubenhauer to call off the hounds, and that includes Fräulein Toller with her short black hair and her athletic build and "with-it night spots," because if she's at the airport, or if I notice *anyone* glance in my direction this weekend with more than passing interest, I'll assume I'm being watched, and start a divorce so nasty it'll end your political ambitions forever in this life and the next.

HUGH: If I talk to him, will you agree to never see this man again?

LINDY: You handle your end; I'll handle mine.

HUGH: I need more than that.

LINDY: Don't we all. It's what we settle for that matters.

HUGH: I want to trust you.

LINDY: Then—*trust me.*

HUGH: Should I trust this new medication that allows you to climax?

LINDY *(Understanding)*: Is *that* why you brought my vanity case down? To slip out the bottle and count pills? Are we becoming people like that?

HUGH: What am I supposed to think when you act all warm and upbeat about your new cocktail, and ask me to come with you this weekend? What if I'd said yes?

LINDY: Say it. Say you'll come with me and I'll book us a larger room, and pack your raincoat, we'll see if Detroit has any big statues to fornicate under.

HUGH: You know I can't do that.

LINDY: Why not?

HUGH *(Seriously considering her proposal)*: Who'd look after Willy?

LINDY: Bring him along. There's a water park in Red Oaks.

HUGH: Steubenhauer organized a strategy retreat for the primary countdown.

LINDY: If you choose me right now, and this I swear, darling, if I rate a weekend with you over all other options, I'll decide to never need anyone else again till the day I die.

HUGH: It's brilliant how you turn it back on me. All night long: the gasping, the moans, the wonderful new meds, except you're not *on* meds, are you? So what am I supposed to make of this loving-wife act: singing in the shower, dancing me around the bedroom—what's making you so happy, is it me, or is it thoughts of your weekend ahead out of town? How can I trust anything you say?

LINDY: Did you count my pills? Did I take my dose? *(They look at each other)* You motherfucker. Get me some water.

(He's gone. Lindy fumbles open her vanity and takes out her pills, loudly commenting on each action for his benefit:)

I'm getting out my pill dispenser. *(Beat)* I'm popping the cap. *(Beat)* I'm pouring the correct dosage into my hand.

(Hugh returns with a glass of water. Lindy extends her flat hand, palm up, so he can see the pills.)

HUGH *(Suddenly affable)*: They look like giant birthday cake sprinkles, don't they.

LINDY: And fuck you, too. *(Pops the pills into her mouth and drinks the water)* Happy?

HUGH *(Lifting her suitcase)*: What on earth are you bringing? The conference is only two days.

LINDY: No Lena. No tan cardigan. Tell Steubenhauer.

HUGH *(Now his rules)*: And you'll remember what's at stake?

(He takes the suitcase outside.
    Lindy spits the pills into her hand and pockets them. She lifts her vanity case, checks herself in her mirror, and with a jaunty flick of her hair, she goes out.)

SCENE 3

The living room is gloomy in half light. The curtains are drawn, shutting out a bright early fall afternoon. A key in the lock. Lindy enters. She looks tan, loose and wonderfully rested, fresh from the perfect vacation. She calls to Hugh outside:

LINDY: My god, it's a mausoleum in here; I told Malka, "*Leave the curtains open when you finish cleaning!*" She knows we're back today, I'm never sure how much she understands with that sideways shrug, and the Dracula smile.

(She throws open the curtains—light bursts in. The foliage outside is of brilliant autumn colors. Mail is heaped on the table. Lindy lifts a handful of it carelessly as Hugh enters, tossing his jacket over a chair. He straightens his umbrella in the stand by the door, then goes back out. Lindy speaks to herself and to Hugh outside:)

(Regarding the mail) One pile, typical. Why is it so difficult for that woman to grasp the concept of one pile for junk mail, one pile for *real* mail.

(Hugh reenters with two large suitcases.)

HUGH *(Regardng the mail)*: Anything important?

LINDY: Let's not be back yet. Let's spend one more night in Cozumel.

HUGH: It was fun, wasn't it.

LINDY: It was everything I dreamed of. We should escape more often, leave the baggage at home and remember who we are without trappings.

HUGH: I booked us the same room next year. I thought we could make it a regular thing.

LINDY: Sweet thoughtful man, that is *so . . . you*. Really, you *are* a good person, Hugh.

HUGH *(Looking at her with real ache)*: Something changed last week. Did you feel it?

LINDY: Of course.

HUGH: I thought it was over, being together with you *that way*. It doesn't go away. Everything is always there, isn't it . . . hiding.

LINDY *(Surprised)*: Am I rubbing off, that sounded almost poetic.

HUGH: I watched people sneak looks at you on Paradise Beach. They see us together and wonder what's my secret, how do I keep a woman like you.

LINDY: When a pretty woman went past, my mother used to say, "There goes someone's problem."

(He comes closer, kisses her. She responds; a whimper of arousal.)

Let's go upstairs.

HUGH: The minute we get home.

LINDY *(Bantering)*: Where are we now? Did we move?

HUGH *(A reminder)*: We have plans.

LINDY: Plans, phooey, I forgot. What pla— *(Remembers)* —Oh.

HUGH: Ruggiero's?

LINDY *(Trying)*: Ruggiero's, right, right.

HUGH *(Smiles)*: I'll take the bags upstairs.

LINDY: Don't touch anything. Don't move. Our last six weeks of private life. Steubenhauer was good to give us this little break before the Big Countdown.

HUGH: He didn't give; I demanded. For *us*.

LINDY *(Watches him for a moment)*: If only we could freeze moments like this—fresh from a vacation, not quite home, waiting to meet our boys for a family dinner at Ruggiero's . . . *"collectables"* to haul out later, not like a photo album to look at, *real 3-D happy times* you could jump inside and reexperience, one after another, skipping the tedium between.

HUGH *(Worried)*: We should freshen up. The boys arrive in a few hours.

LINDY: Of course. Let's "freshen up." Let's drive to Ruggiero's and meet our children and have dinner. Let's do all those things.

HUGH: We're meeting here first, remember?

LINDY: Oh. Do I? Yes, that's right.

HUGH: It's a two-hour-plus bus ride from St. Andrew's, they'll want to shower and change before we eat.

LINDY *(After a brief look at him)*: You know what? Why drive all the way downtown for dinner on our first night home? Let's order in Mexican and eat sloppy joes in the den.

HUGH: I made reservations, Lindy. Over a month ago. You don't cancel on Carmine Ruggiero. *(Beat)* I'll take the luggage upstairs.

LINDY *(Puzzled)*: A reservation? We have a permanent table by the lobster tank. And why would the boys have to *change* for Carmine? He let them park their skateboards in the kitchen, even last spring.

HUGH *(With patience)*: Is it a problem?

(She studies him a moment.)

LINDY *(Understanding)*: Oh. *(After a moment)* I thought we agreed you'd stop doing this.

HUGH: Eating out?

LINDY: Be straight with me: "I promised Steubenhauer a family portrait at Ruggiero's," then you won't have to go through a whole charade when the photographer pretends to be passing through the restaurant and happens to have a camera in his car right outside in the parking lot, and as long as he's there wouldn't it be great to do a "family portrait," or however you set it up. And I wouldn't have to worry that I might be losing what's left of my mind—because I can't recall a plan I never knew about in the first place.

HUGH: I told Luther's photographer he could have ten minutes, that's it. No assistants. No lights. I didn't want it hanging over our return. *(Beat)* I apologize? *(He feels guilty)*

LINDY *(Unfazed; musing)*: Doug's nose ring, and the scorpion tattoo on his neck?

HUGH: They have inspection before they're allowed on the bus home, remember?

LINDY: If they're on it . . .

HUGH: How else would they get home . . .

LINDY: The Mustang.

HUGH: That car's to work on, to learn engine maintenance . . . that's the agreement up there.

LINDY: They're sons of privilege. Rules don't apply to them.

HUGH *(Friendly, controlled)*: If you're looking for things to worry about, I can start a list.

LINDY (*Appraising his certainty*): How'd your people organize all—do gremlins from Steubenhauer call them at school, "*No body jewelry, kids, we're going for the classic-preppy look, orders from Mission Command?*" Did they buy the boys a wardrobe? (*Wry smile*) Do we have a stylist?

(*Hugh is silent.*)

Lord help me. I was joking! (*Absorbing this*) Isn't there a way to keep the children out of our political charade?

HUGH: It's time they learned to play at the Big Table.

LINDY (*A recognition*): He never called, my Dougie-Bug. I'm always the first one he talks to— (*Oh!*) Did they warn him not to? Did you?

HUGH: He can't come crying to Mommy every time he's asked to pull his weight.

LINDY (*Disbelief*): He *was* warned!

HUGH: Both of them were fully briefed.

LINDY: Without me. In case I took it badly?

HUGH (*With legal precision*): A lot of factors to weigh here.

LINDY (*With utter calm*): So it's your agenda all the way now. (*Steeling herself*) Fine. Just don't orchestrate our life behind my back. I can handle anything you throw at me.

HUGH: From now on, full disclosure. You have my word.

LINDY (*Appeased*): I think *white* for Ruggiero's. Something just-back-from-the-sun to offset my sumptuous tan.

HUGH (*With love and appreciation*): Sometimes I forget how quickly you understand. I know you've given up a great deal for me . . .

LINDY (*Gently*): Shhh, Hugh.

HUGH: Feelings are important to you, I know that . . . all the stuff inside—poetry! I wish I knew why people . . . what they find so interesting about basically / noises in your head. They are just a distraction as far as I can see—you can't make use of it, so what's the point?

LINDY (*Amused*): *What* indeed?!

HUGH (*Trying*): Maybe some people just have bigger feelings than others? Something like that?

LINDY (*Playful and warm*): *Maybe.*

HUGH: *Mucho mas?*

LINDY (*Smiling*): *Mucho!*

HUGH (*Vulnerable*): I watch you with the boys, in the kitchen, jabbering away over breakfast. I always figured, "Sons! They'll be my pals." But it turns out they're more . . . (*Not sure*) . . . The smart-mouth stuff is all from *you* . . . I see you all together and I think, "I gave them this home, I made them safe and happy, that's what I'm supposed to do . . . that should be enough . . ." But I never know— with you three, I never know. (*Not sure where he's going with this; he almost loses it*)

LINDY (*Tenderly*): Is a drink indicated?

(*Beat. An awkward moment.*)

HUGH: That blue package on the table should be for you. (*She looks, finds a padded envelope*) Mexican postage.

LINDY (*Reading the return address*): Cozumel? (*Beat*) What on earth . . . ?

HUGH: Open it.

(*She opens the envelope and finds a narrow box inside.*)

You kept sneaking back down to the hotel gift shop for a peek.

LINDY (*Holding up a necklace*): Oh, Hugh! This isn't the one—

HUGH (*Puzzled for a moment*): Crud-monkey, they screwed up . . .

LINDY: "Crud-monkey"?

HUGH: I explained three times, wrote instructions, I even watched them wrap the damn thing.

LINDY *(Glossing over the mishap)*: It's *much* better than what I wanted: "A mistake that read my mind."

HUGH *(Lightening, segueing into an almost political speech with a friendly audience)*: "I knew those people would botch it. How can they expect to build a service economy when the point-of-contact laborer doesn't take more pride in his work?" I'll send it back.

LINDY *(Reading the note)*: "Darling, Smutty-Witch. Yours always, Hugh." *(Moved)* I'll wear it tonight.

HUGH *(A puzzling outburst)*: No! *(More calm)* Your neck is so perfect, why ruin it with jewelry.

(She kisses him. Hugh carries the luggage upstairs. Lindy's eyes linger on him quizzically until he is gone. Her thoughts racing, she replaces the necklace in its box, eyeing it with an uneasy feeling. Finally, she speed-dials her phone.)

LINDY *(Into the phone, giggling)*: Right first time—is that psychic powers, or caller ID? *(Beat)* Yes, a few minutes ago. It was very sweet and tender, and now it's turning complicated. *(Listens)* —No, Adam, I can't start a divorce till he's in office, the scandal would be—they'd drag the kids in. *(Listens)* Yes, that's the big one. I dread that conversation—even when we have the high ground our kids think we're a joke. *(Listens)* No, don't pretend what we're doing is *good* for anyone. If we'd met years ago, we'd be in amazing luck . . . But we didn't, and what we want now is bad, we'll cause pain . . . it can't be helped, and that's all there is to it. Patience, my love.

(She hangs up. Hugh has returned. It isn't clear if he has heard any of the call. He checks his watch, and then her.)

HUGH *(Appraisingly)*: You're breathtaking.

LINDY *(Surprised)*: Thank you.

HUGH: You're a witch.

LINDY *(Gauging the innuendo)*: A *smutty* one?

HUGH: Change for dinner.

LINDY: Will you watch?

HUGH *(Approaching her)*: Come here.

(He starts to unbutton her blouse. She is instantly aroused—soft high yelps.)

Do you love me?

(They make love. Their arousal is immediate and complete as they sink down on the couch and the lights grow dim, shadowy.

Time passes.

Hugh rises slowly, buttoning his shirt. He turns the light on, the room grows brighter. Lindy's asleep on the couch. Hugh studies her for a long time. He wants to touch her again, to stay like this forever. Finally, he checks his watch.)

(Gently) Lindy. *(Shakes her)* You have to get ready, the boys'll be here any minute. *(Stroking her skin)* Like silk.

(She makes mumble-sleep sounds. He sits beside her.)

I smell beach. No . . . suntan lotion. *(Beat)* Are you asleep? *(To her, with wonder)* How do you throw yourself at everything without—aren't you afraid of pain? Of danger? Of anything?

(Lindy murmurs again in her sleep.)

Are you listening? It would be so *you* to fake sleep, get me talking when I think you can't hear. *I* hear things when you don't know . . .

(One racking sob escapes him, then he's quickly back in control.)

Never leave me.

(Lindy stirs, smiles, wakes, looks at Hugh, in a postcoital languor.)

LINDY: Oh, Hugh, look what you did to me; I'm all spongy and well copulated. What a good spongy-wife-maker you are.

HUGH *(Flat)*: Time to get dressed.

(She studies him.)

LINDY *(Breezily)*: I loved our vacation. Thank you. And I loved my gift.

HUGH: Good.

LINDY: I wish I wasn't so complicated.

HUGH: We're cutting it a little close, Lindy.

LINDY *(Lovingly)*: Do you know how much I appreciate, *respect* your approach to—to everything? When life gets dangerous you flee the storms of New York and steer us to safety. You give us shelter and peace of mind. Truly, you're the captain of my ship . . .

HUGH *(Growing uneasy)*: Where are you going with this?

LINDY: Shhh, Hugh. You're wonderful, that's all / that's all I want to say. If we had daughters, I'd want them to marry a man like you.

HUGH *(Erupting, contradictory emotions tumbling out)*: But we have *sons*, Lindy. And one day they'll have to carry on the family name. A beautiful woman like you can indulge your fancy flights. Sure, when you spin out of control there's always someone nearby to catch you! Men don't have that luxury—we crash, we burn. If I don't teach my sons to take care of the business, the way I was taught—

LINDY (*Startled and confused, she tries to soothe*): Your masculinity is widely noted within—and without—the family unit.

HUGH: You think I grew tired of New York, and Father's death was a handy excuse to pack it in?

LINDY: Time to get dressed!

(*She starts out. He takes her harshly by the arm.*)

HUGH: You stay right here.

LINDY: Hugh!

HUGH: Do you have *any* idea what I've given up for you?

LINDY: Let go of me—

HUGH (*Oblivious*): I made International Banking the most profitable division in thirty-eight years. That's right, me, with no experience, nothing, I just got it, I was a natural. My boss, when I gave notice, he offered to triple my salary, triple, Lindy, three times the ridiculous fortune I already made, plus stock options, mortgage covered, both boys' private education paid through graduate school . . . I was kicking major ass in that bank and I didn't give it up because Dad was dead and the Pedal Empire had no King, I gave it up because I wanted you more.

LINDY: You had me, Hugh. I was happy in New York . . .

HUGH: While your arty friends made a fuss over that book of yours, sure . . . but what does that mean. It's all just opinions, how do you make sure someone's good; I took your poems to an old friend at Columbia . . .

LINDY: Oh god, not the giant embryo-person with the wobbly chin?!

HUGH: "Emotional flailing by yet another over-educated Sylvia Plath wannabe," that's what he said.

LINDY: Everyone in New York knows he's a fraud—you decided our future based on his opinion? Not on *my excitement*? Or even that review in the *Village Voice*? Or just . . . faith in me?

HUGH: There is a bigger picture here, Lindy. What if you weren't a real poet? What if New York had the final word and it told you you weren't as good as your fancy friends were saying? And your condition got worse, which everyone said it might. If you broke down, what would happen to the boys, to our family? I had to make a choice. If I was wrong . . . and I've often wondered about that. God help me if I did the wrong thing, but I gave up a great deal—for *us*. And now you'll do the same.

(He goes up the stairs.
Lindy finds her poetry book in a small bookcase and starts to flip through it.
The landline rings. Lindy answers and listens.)

LINDY *(Into the phone)*: No, it's his wife. *(Beat)* He's here. *(Beat)*. A green Mustang? No, that can't be right, they're on a bus. *(Beat)* How would I know the license number, is there a problem?

(She listens and grows utterly still. Hugh returns, sensing that something is wrong.)

HUGH: Who is it? *(Beat)* Lindy?

(He pries the phone from her hand. Lindy remains eerily immobile.)

Hugh Metz speaking, can I help you? *(Beat. Becoming very still)* I see. Where are they now? *(Beat)* Give us twenty minutes, thank you. *(He hangs up)*
    Lindy?

(She doesn't respond.)

Be strong now. The boys will need us. Do you understand what happened?

LINDY *(Simply)*: Yes.

HUGH: St. Eustace has the best trauma unit downstate.

LINDY: That's good, right? *(Trying to rally, calmly)* You should call Steubenhauer.

HUGH: Later.

LINDY: No. His people need to contact the doctors, make a plan to dodge the press.

HUGH: Why?

LINDY: The Metz boys driving home under the influence, are you kidding?

HUGH: The police didn't say anything about—what did they tell you?

LINDY: You need a diagram? The two of them leaving for the weekend in Willy's Mustang convertible—convertible, oh god, no roll bar . . .

(He holds her tightly, both for control and for solace.)

HUGH: Focus, Melinda. I can't do this without you.

LINDY *(Freeing herself)*: They were instructed how to dress for dinner with their parents. Told not to call Mother. They saw the future—*of course they were stoned.*

HUGH: Please don't pull this crazy shit on me—focus.

LINDY *(Trying to control a severe emotional skid)*: Yes. Sorry. I'm a little upset. It seems my boys are lying unconscious in a trauma center—

HUGH: Hot shower. Hot as you can make it, then . . . hospital. I'll wait here, I need time to think.

LINDY: Steubenhauer should hear the news from you first. Warn him to put his best people on the cover-up. Show him you think fast under pressure.

HUGH: I'll just . . . sit for a second. Get my focus. We can call from the car.

LINDY: Dozens of people worked to put you where you are. This is no time to stumble. Call Steubenhauer.

HUGH: Yes. Okay. I'll just . . . I'll call him.

LINDY: I'll tell Ruggiero I decided to cook or something. Bring a notepad for the drive, we'll plan damage control. *(Her calm is unnatural, too controlled)*

HUGH: Would you like to change?

LINDY *(Puzzled)*: Change? Oh, *clothing* . . . I thought you meant "into someone else"!!! *(Brief laugh)* Dark colors. Trauma ward, yes. Black will be good if we lose one.

HUGH *(Alarmed by her eerie calm)*: Lindy?

LINDY: That was pessimistic! *(A stupid-silly voice)* "Crud-monkey!" We want an upbeat message! Does Steubenhauer have a playbook for candidates who lose a child? Or both? Find out if we're allowed to grieve without spin if that happens. Hugh, phone your boss, be a good Hugh, woof-woof.

(She leaves.
Hugh speed-dials Steubenhauer.)

HUGH *(With nervous glances upstairs toward Lindy)*: Lute it's me. I have some very bad news.

(Spine-chilling screams from upstairs that build and build relentlessly. The screams turn into the sounds of a wounded animal. Then we hear a crash—a large object being thrown violently.)

(Into the phone; jolted) I'll have to get back to you. *(He hangs up)*

(Lindy's moaning continues with violent crashing sounds, as Hugh runs up the stairs, calling out:)

I'm here, Lindy. I'm coming.

(The lights dim.)

SCENE 4

Lindy stands in the open front doorway surveying the living room. She looks depleted and frail.

It's four days later. The front window is boarded up, a broken chair is stacked in a corner, and the torn curtains have been pinned together carelessly.

Hugh enters the house, holding an overnight suitcase and Mexican take-out. He stands beside Lindy. Both stare at the room.

LINDY: I did this?

HUGH: Can I get you water? Juice?

LINDY: How bad was I? On a scale of ninety-nine to a hundred?

(Hugh closes the front door.)

HUGH: Don't worry about it.

LINDY: *Worry?* I can't even *remember*— *(Baffled)* I'm sure
I took my meds, I don't understand—? *[what happened]*
HUGH: Stressful news.

(Beat.)

LINDY *(Focusing)*: Can I see my children now?
HUGH: Of course; we'll freshen up, I'll call the hospital, and—
LINDY: Did they ask why I haven't been to visit?
HUGH: It's only four days, the first two were intensive care.
LINDY *(With more focus)*: You'd tell me if— *(She stops)*
HUGH: It's a miracle there was so little trauma.
LINDY: I'm so sorry, Hugh.
HUGH: Rest. Get your strength back. You wanted to see the
boys. Dr. Vine let you out early, but you promised you'd
eat and stick to a schedule.

(He starts to the kitchen. She doesn't move.)

LINDY: Bring some plates in here. I want to remind myself
how dangerous I am. *(Beat)* . . . The boys are really—?
HUGH *(Stops her)*: They're fine, Lindy. They'll be released
early next week.
LINDY: Can they talk? I'd like to hear them. I can handle it.
HUGH: Eat first. Then I'll call. Then we'll drive straight to St.
Eustace if you feel ready.
LINDY: I'd like that very much.

(Lindy's watch alarm goes off.)

Time for the yellow ones! Could you bring me water?

*(She removes pills from her handbag. He exits with the
take-out.)*

(Lindy speed-dials her cell phone. She waits for an answer, then speaks quietly, checking that Hugh hasn't returned. Beat.)

I tried to reach you last night—

(Beat.)

I *do* want to talk, but—

(She listens a long time, then looks to make sure she is still alone.)

I'm not *avoiding* you, other things need attention right now. *(Listens)* Even if he left me, what future could there be for us when we started in lies and deception. Please let go, Adam . . .

(She ends the call, fighting a sudden wave of nausea. Hugh comes forward with a glass of water.)

(Taking the glass) Thank you. No one's been 'round to fix the damage?

HUGH: Not yet.

LINDY: Isn't Steubenhauer concerned?

HUGH: We haven't discussed it.

LINDY: Where'd you stay while I—?

HUGH *(A faint grin)*: Mama Metz.

LINDY *(More puzzled)*: We don't want passersby to see the window boarded up, I'll call the builder, it's time this place got a makeover—

HUGH *(Carefully)*: The clinic has a news blackout for patients. There's things you'll be starting to hear about.

LINDY: Shit. Did they leave the boys out of it?

HUGH: Yes . . . airbrushed by the police: driving under age. *(Beat)* St. Andrew's will take them back on probation when they're . . . ready. With counseling, and random drug tests. They can't keep a car at school.

(Beat.)

LINDY: So my meltdown was—epic?

HUGH *(Beat)*: *People* magazine's pulling your piece.

LINDY: "Bipolar Wives with Second Careers" is too small a demographic for their readership? They might be surprised.

HUGH: My campaign's over. I withdrew.

LINDY *(Beat)*: Why?

HUGH: Save Lute the awkwardness.

LINDY: Oh, Hugh.

HUGH: You never took it all that seriously . . . be honest.

LINDY: But *you* did. And if you had that, I'd be . . .

HUGH: You'd be . . . *what?*

LINDY: It doesn't matter.

HUGH *(Ruefully)*: When the boys heard I quit the race, Doug texted me from the hospital: "It's okay, Pop, we still have *South Park* for laughs." If I ever talked to my father that way! Did you find it comical—me running for office?

LINDY: Oh, Hugh, who cares what I think, I'm the loony wife who ruined your career! *(Almost in tears)* Can you ever forgive me?

HUGH: It's no use feeling sorry for ourselves.

LINDY: We hit bottom. I want to salvage what's left.

HUGH *(On edge)*: Would you like a nap before we start downstate?

LINDY: Do you think we could forget each other's stupid mistakes and move on?

HUGH *(Uneasy)*: I'll just change while you freshen up.

(Lindy's phone rings.)

LINDY *(Ignoring the phone)*: Let's redo this room. Bright colors, like Cozumel. We'll wake up every day the way we—

HUGH: Who just called?

LINDY *(Dismissive)*: Everyone wants me since I returned. It's hell being popular . . .

(The phone rings a few more times. Both are still. It stops.)

HUGH: Check the ID.

LINDY *(Beat)*: We'll talk tonight. After we see the boys.

HUGH: You saw him at the conference. And several times after. Adam Penzius?

LINDY: Didn't we agree this topic was off-limits?

HUGH: Steubenhauer gave me a box of documents when I withdrew from the race.

LINDY *(Beat)*: It was Adam, yes.

HUGH: He's your lover.

LINDY: He's my . . . he *was* a friend.

HUGH: There were photographs. *(Beat)* I didn't look.

LINDY *(Studying him)*: Hugh, I can't ask you to forgive—or *understand*—what I've done. Just . . . can we give it time to settle before we . . . before—

HUGH: Why did you need him?

LINDY: I have to handle one thing at a time. *(Controlling herself)* Let's visit the boys—

HUGH: Leave them out of this.

LINDY: Leave them out? Look at this room, Hugh. This is what I do. "Hurricane-Lindy." My gift to the younger generation.

HUGH: Don't go slip-slidy on me, I asked a question.

LINDY *(Calm)*: Slip-slidy is not this, Hugh. It's pretending a few pills will put things right, and, with luck, maybe my *condition* will bypass the boys, right? . . . Well, I don't know if it will. And you don't know. Look at the uncertainty I've asked you to live with, and you ask so little in return. I needed Adam—I realized this at the clinic—he was my "in case." *In case* you got fed up and did the understandable thing.

HUGH: My god, listen to you.

LINDY: It's nothing I'm proud of. I'm not strong like you, not *that* way. I need . . . *(Thinks)* I want you. I want the life we made. If you can ever forgive me.

HUGH: I don't think you have any idea how thoroughly repellent you are to me right now.

LINDY *(Confused)*: Hugh?

HUGH: You ripped my life to shreds. You played me. And now, true to form, when you're fragile and needy, out comes the eleventh-hour emotional blackmail. "I'm not proud of myself . . . Can you ever forgive me?"

LINDY *(Trying to hold on)*: What can I do to prove—?

HUGH: Nothing. What I'd like—the thing I want most of all right now is for you to have never happened. I'd like to take back every minute from the day we met. I want to feel what it's like to live life with someone fucking normal.

LINDY *(Shocked)*: What?

HUGH: I'm sick of being married to a crazy person, Lindy. I'm sick of how you undermine all my efforts to get our life on track. I'm sick of your insane need to confuse being special with the plain truth that you're just a fucked-up woman—that's all—a fucked-up person who's infected everything and everyone around her. I'm sick of, of . . . *(He's choking up, then stops himself; getting it together)* . . . of your evil power over everything, you overwhelm— *(He stops again)*

LINDY *(Apologetic)*: Oh, Hugh . . . I so understand.

HUGH: *You have no idea!!!* You tangle everything in knots, then run to Crazy Land and disappear. When I turn in the drive at night my heart pounds. I never know which Lindy I'll find in my house—

LINDY *(Approaching him with sympathy)*: Oh, poor baby—

HUGH *(Nearly unhinged)*: Stay over there. Don't come towards me.

LINDY *(With sympathy)*: I shouldn't inflict myself on people.

HUGH: Do you *love* him?

LINDY: It's over.

HUGH: We should be settled by now. We should be able to rely on each other. The factory's holding on by a hair. My boys are badly hurt. I can't concentrate, I have so many things to deal with, and no help from . . . from—

LINDY: I'll take my pills, Hugh. I'll get fat, or skinny, and tremble, or lie around like a slug—whatever the next combo of pills does to me I'll live with it for your sake, but please remember who made this life of ours work . . . You have a home everyone envies. It's your only complete success.

HUGH: I've found someone. I'm leaving you.

(Lindy freezes. She feels the inevitability of this instantly. Her mind races through a dozen scenarios.)

LINDY *(Can't resist a bitter dig)*: Did Steubenhauer know?

HUGH: It's his intern. Lena Toller.

LINDY *(Utter disbelief)*: The girl from the conference? My assistant? She's sixteen!

HUGH: She's thirty-three, actually. She looks young.

LINDY *(Steadying herself)*: Let's visit the boys, then talk afterwards.

HUGH: This isn't a conversation. It's a bulletin. I'm leaving.

LINDY *(Screams)*: I HEARD YOU. I DESERVE IT. WHAT TOOK YOU SO LONG?!

HUGH: Please, Lindy—

LINDY *(Forcing self-control)*: There will be no scenes! *(Almost stoic)* I never imagined you with someone else, not really "with"—*fucking*, yes, but *bonding*? Why is that? Even when you used that stupid word: "*Crud-monkey*"! It's hers, isn't it? When did all this start?—

HUGH: A while ago. We'll marry as soon as our divorce is final. I hope you won't make a fuss.

LINDY *(Amazed)*: Adam and I were planning to run off together the moment you won office. I felt so rotten about it.

HUGH: The papers are on your desk. If you refuse, it might turn ugly.

LINDY: Why am I the betrayer, when you've been seeing this little pop tart since "a while back." How did this all become so one-sided?

HUGH *(Mock innocence)*: Seeing who?

LINDY: My Personal Shopper. Lena Crud-Monkey.

HUGH *(Enacting his "position")*: Steubenhauer's intern? Where did you hear that? She's a sweet kid, but her and me?—

LINDY: You just told me— *(Catching on)* My god, *I'm* starting to feel like the healthy one.

HUGH: Some people scream when they hurt. Others . . . *plan.*

LINDY *(A moment of helpless disbelief; then pounding his chest violently)*: You'll never find another woman like me.

HUGH *(Holding her wrists)*: Control yourself.

LINDY: I'm the only risk you ever took, without me nothing about you is courageous.

HUGH: I've decided. There's no discussion.

LINDY: Do yourself a favor, tell her it's off. You'll have nothing to talk about when the intrigue ends, when she's your wife. We've shared a whole life together; this is our little Crazy Land—Lena's hitchhiking with a day pass and no map, shit, she doesn't even know the exchange rate around here.

HUGH: Shall I call the hospital?

LINDY: Why do you always, *always*, settle for less than you are.

HUGH: No one's listening, Melinda. Get ready. The boys expect us.

(Hugh moves off to call the hospital.

Lindy sits perfectly still for a moment. Her body shudders. Then she's still again.

She removes her compact and calmly applies makeup.

The lights dim.)

SCENE 5

A bright spring morning, very early. The curtains are open wide, light streaming in. Gentle rockabilly from a small radio plays. Major redecoration is underway: a drop cloth and newspapers are spread on the floor; there are paint trays, rollers, a toolbox, etc. The mood is light, the start of a day when everything ahead holds promise.

An unshaven Hugh unlocks the front door and enters, wearing jogging shorts and a Metz Bicycles T-shirt.

He tries to appear relaxed, but his awkwardness shows.

HUGH: Lindy? *(No answer)* Melinda? *(Louder, over the music)* Anyone home?

(Lindy enters in paint-splattered coveralls, paint flecks on her face, holding a paint roller, her hair pinned up under a house-painter's cap. She looks more beautiful than ever, at

peace with herself for the first time . . . starting to accept a
future that's hers alone.

She regards Hugh in silence for a moment, as if she
can't quite recall who he is.)

You didn't change the locks? *(No response)* Isn't that
Doug's Camry down the street?

LINDY *(Coolly)*: Probably.

HUGH: What happened to his Colorado intern thing?

LINDY: Change of plan; he's helping me get the house ready
to show.

HUGH: Could you . . . *(Regarding the music; she turns it down)*
You're selling?

LINDY: There's just me now. It's impractical. And there's
professional considerations . . . places I applied to teach.

HUGH: I didn't know.

LINDY: Several made offers. My article caused quite a stir.

HUGH: Congratulations.

LINDY *(Genuinely)*: Thank you.

(Hugh wanders the room, taking it in. Spotting the
newspapers underfoot, he leans over, reading. Lindy sees
what he's found:)

That headline's my favorite: "Whacky Wife Topples
Bike Biggie." The press is too kind. Never mind, at least
the paper's finally serving a purpose . . . protecting the
floor from paint . . . Whoops, my "imaginary-audience."
Pull up a chair, Hugh, I'm off meds, the entertainment's
nonstop.

(Hugh continues to wander, passing the table. He sees a
stack of magazines neatly piled, multiple copies of the
same issue.)

HUGH *(Taking one off the top, holding it up)*: I read your article. *(Beat)* Lena bought the magazine. *(Beat)* She found it interesting.

LINDY: And what did *Hugh* find it?

HUGH *(Unfazed)*: Kinda technical. Psychology's not my thing . . .

LINDY: It's a professional journal, Hugh. For specialists. Who'd have thought technical prose was my *forte*.

HUGH *(Beat)*: May I talk to Doug?

LINDY: He's not here.

HUGH: His car's out front.

LINDY: They're using May-Lin's.

HUGH: "May-Lin"?

LINDY: Current squeeze.

HUGH: Since when?

LINDY: Two weeks. *(Smirks)* In teen time that's about the length of our marriage.

HUGH *(Beat)*: Don't sell now, Lindy. Mortgage rates are dropping—I'll get you a much better price if you wait for—

LINDY: Taking care of my finances belongs to another time. Our present situation demands new behaviors—you may even have to stop dropping by in mid-jog— *(Checking her watch)* before seven A.M.

(Hugh starts to pace. It's clear he has something on his mind and can't decide how to begin.)

Could you stop wandering . . . or wander and talk at the same time if something's on your mind.

HUGH: I noticed on the way past—maybe you're not aware there's a water watch. *(Starts to explain)* Tuesday's dry this side of the street.

LINDY *(Smiles)*: Is it?

HUGH: Your sprinkler was on.

LINDY *(With relish)*: My sprinkler?

HUGH: Yes. It was . . .

LINDY: Sprinkling? Thanks for the warning. Was there anything else?

HUGH *(Trying to ease the indefinable tension)*: Where'd Doug sleep last night?

LINDY: At May-Lin's. Or in her new Hummer; a present from her parents for getting a C+ in chemistry.

HUGH: Is he . . . *careful* with her?

LINDY *(Confused)*: Careful?

HUGH: . . . During intimacy?

LINDY *(Amused)*: When you and Doug are on speaking terms again you should ask him to do "Dad's condom lecture." He may put it on YouTube.

HUGH *(Prickly)*: I don't think thirteen was too young to discuss the facts of life. *(She guffaws)* Okay, laugh if you will, but there's a reality here, and someone has to tell my boys what's what.

LINDY: The "reality" *is* that Doug lost his virginity when he was twelve. To his roommate at the weight-watcher's camp we made him attend, so you could walk tall with your hard-body alpha-male buds.

HUGH: Roommate? A boy?

LINDY: Welcome to your family. Don't worry, he's decided he prefers girls on the whole. *(Laughs)* That was funny; he prefers the "whole" of girls. All their "holes." Thank you, Audience.

HUGH *(Suddenly)*: Lena's pregnant.

LINDY *(Startled, despite herself)*: By you?

HUGH: I thought you should hear it from me.

(Lindy starts checking color samples.)

We're getting married early next month.

LINDY: I thought conception was only possible *after* puberty.

HUGH: The rest of the town has age jokes covered.

LINDY: You expect a better class of insult from me? I'm flattered.

HUGH: Mother thinks a small ceremony. I agree. I'd like the kids there. And you, too, but, of course . . . I'll understand if you—

LINDY: If I . . . what?

HUGH: She and Doug have issues. I think he doesn't like her. *(Beat)* Has he *said* anything to you?

LINDY: He has, yes.

HUGH: Anything I should know about?

LINDY: You want a political answer, or the truth?

HUGH: That bad?

LINDY: He's my *son*, darling. Words are his weapon of choice.

HUGH: At least Willy's being a sport. I'd like them to both be there. If Doug asks . . . please encourage him to come. It would mean a lot.

LINDY *(With a grin)*: She's guilt-tripping you already?! *"Hugh, I think Doug doesn't like me, I feel so bad about it, can you talk to him?"*

HUGH: She doesn't manipulate. We discuss things. Work out our differences *together*. All in all I think she's been pretty outstanding with the boys . . .

LINDY: "The sports-cunt with the jackpot smile"? That's Doug's description. Imagine what he'd say if she wasn't so outstanding with him.

HUGH: She's being as patient as anyone could ask.

LINDY: Oh for fuck's sake, Hugh, who is she to be patient about anything?! This is *our* family. She's an intruder. She *should* feel hated. She *is* hated.

HUGH: More overreaction. Thank you for not disappointing me.

LINDY *(Sudden change)*: You look so damn unhappy.

HUGH: Eye of the beholder. I feel tip-top.

LINDY: "Tip-top"? Is that Lena-speak?

HUGH: I'm running the Chicago Marathon this October. I haven't had so much energy since high school.

LINDY: Don't strain the mechanism for her sake. I'm sure you'll find her interest—*migratory*.

HUGH: She's not at all like you think, Lindy.

LINDY: For your sake I hope not.

HUGH: She's a very domestic person, really. She bakes . . . reads a lot. Even poetry. She found your book online.

LINDY: God no, *The Jock and Gillian Cycle?*

HUGH: She said—let me get this right—"It's wonderfully raw."

LINDY: I'm glad my work has found favor with Young Adult Readers.

HUGH: Do I really look—

LINDY: *Dim* . . . you look / you always had a vitality, a *glow*. You seem *flickery*.

HUGH: Would you tell me what you think about— *(Stops, then reflects)* Funny you're still the one I trust to be completely honest. I'm in sort of a pickle.

LINDY *(Delighted)*: "A pickle"?

(He laughs with her, then almost seems to lose it. She approaches him and ruffles his hair affectionately.)

Poor Pickle-Man. I'm all ears.

HUGH: She's leaving the baby decision to me—to have it; or not.

LINDY: And you want from me *what? Advice?*

HUGH: Impressions. Advice. Yeah.

LINDY *(Beat)*: Buy an elephant gun and blow the bitch away. Is my *advice*. The stupidest woman alive can see you're a man who *does the right thing*. It's entrapment, Hugh. Like I did when I let you plant a baby. Look how *we* turned out.

HUGH: You think it's a mistake?

LINDY: It's her "widdle-wombie." If she let you "hit raw," as my Special Ed kids put it—and if one of her pearly eggs popped a bloom, why then, she made herself a "wee-pwobwem." After she decides what to do, *that's* when she should tell you, not before.

HUGH: I came by to—

LINDY *(Grasps his drift immediately)*: Oh. That's a different pickle altogether.

HUGH: Have you eaten? You were always ravenous in the morning.

(She looks at him for a long time.)

LINDY: How you gonna keep 'em down on the farm.

HUGH: Meaning? *(Getting it)* Oh. Now that I've been with you . . . Yeah, I guess you come to *like* feeling a little off-balance with someone. Addictive, right? *(Beat)* Things were like this sometimes, weren't they. Really nice.

LINDY *(A side-step)*: I'll encourage our sons to attend your wedding. Maybe I'll attend myself . . . bring a little present for Lena-Barbie—the jewelry you meant for her! Did she hate mine as much as I hated hers? Did she throw up her little "fingies" in the air: *(Her fingers in the air, a devastating imitation of Lena aghast)* "Oh, Hugh—*crud-monkey*!"

HUGH *(Halting, off-balance, as if addressing a woman he doesn't know too well)*: Do you still see—

LINDY *(A coy challenge)*: Forgot his name?

HUGH: Adam.

LINDY: *See* him? "Make smutty," you mean? *(Making a connection)* "Smutty-Witch"—my god, on the note with the wrong necklace—is that what you call Lena, too?!

HUGH: Pet names are tough.

LINDY *(Offhand)*: Does she like you inside her? Does she make little yelps, the way I used to— *(She stops, her distress starting to show)*

HUGH: I'm not really comfortable with this conversation.

LINDY: That's why you're here, isn't it? The danger?

HUGH: You *are* seeing him.

LINDY: Ask Steubenhauer to hire a tail if it's so important.

HUGH: I googled his name. He's a pretty big deal.

LINDY: You thought I couldn't do better than a small-town grandee like you? *(Quickly)* That was harsh, sorry. The meds *do* soften my edges, I guess. There's a luxury in solitude, no-one-around-to-behave-for. If I knew you were coming I'd have popped a pill.

HUGH: This is so fucked-up.

LINDY: It's an ex-marriage, it's completely fucking typical. And in case you think I'm indifferent to your recent life—I know Lena-Barbie's uncle is *The* Hunter Gerhardt, major heat in Washington. And not some pathetic, elected fuckable, he's real power, *behind the scenes* where they unwrap the politicians and put the batteries in. Lena's his darling, you know. She's a shrewd move for you.

HUGH: I'm done with politics. It's a rumor, all that comeback talk.

LINDY: The only rumor in your life is reality. You dream when you're awake: politics, power, reputation—all smoke. With luck it'll keep your mind off the stuff that haunts you: Me. Your marriage. The faltering company.

(She has drifted somewhere. Hugh is mesmerized.)

HUGH: How's bacon-egg sandwiches. Tea with lemon. I could pick up something at the mini mall by the Oakville overpass . . .

LINDY *(Beat)*: Does Lena know you're using her? Does she understand it's her connections that get you hard.

HUGH: Don't, Lindy.

LINDY: "It's-not-true" don't or "I-don't-want-to-hear-it" don't.

HUGH: Lena understands what's expected. It's her world.

LINDY: And her chemicals behave when you turn the heat up.

HUGH: Will you have breakfast with me or not?

LINDY *(Tenderly)*: And of course she never saw your nerve fail when you tried to break from your family, or watch the company sink—in spite of all your heroic efforts—or feel your humiliation, pretending Steubenhauer didn't smell a wounded beast he could tame and ride. She doesn't know that side of you.

HUGH *(Simply)*: There were times—back then—

LINDY *(Tenderly)*: I'm sorry, that was harsh.

HUGH *(Beat)*: I bought a gun.

LINDY: In the garage, I know, baby. I hid the bullets.

HUGH *(Watching her with painful desire)*: When I'm with you—right now—I think, if I told Lena it was all a mistake. If I asked you to dinner?

LINDY *(Singing)*: "They paved paradise, and put up a parking lot."

HUGH *(Moving close to her)*: I've tried to stay away.

(They kiss. It grows intense . . .)

LINDY: Careful, baby, you know how fast I go *ding* off meds . . . *(Backing away, agitated, pacing)*

HUGH *(Nervous)*: If I were to visit you from time to time . . . would you find that acceptable?

LINDY *(Amused)*: When we were married, you didn't want to know. Now you can't live without it—how's a gal to keep up?

HUGH: I thought leaving you would solve everything. It's nothing like I imagined.

LINDY: Listen to me, Hugh. Listen and hear my words. I'm moving.

HUGH: There's a brand-new development in Chester, I could get you an early bid—

LINDY: Away from this city, this place. I'm going home, maybe—North Carolina. Or Texas, my cousins there. Maybe—New York?

HUGH: Could we discuss this?

LINDY: No discussion—it's a "bulletin."

HUGH: Why, Lindy—

LINDY: There's nothing left for me here.

HUGH: Why'd you have to fuck this Adam Penzius?

LINDY *(Sharp)*: Why'd you have to fuck Toddler-Lena? No, why couldn't you *just* fuck her and be done with it. I slept with Adam because—who knows why—because I wanted to, I needed to, why do people do stupid things? But I'd never throw my life away like you've done, and like you're trying to half undo with this appeal to Wife-One to stay put and play Pit-Stop-Mama whenever you're up for a Sunrise Quickie. You've chosen some child to share your bed, her story starts at the end of yours—she's a stranger. And if I meet some vigorous old poop who can crank out a few good times before the lights go dim, *and* if we manage to grow close in our daffy old way, even then we won't share a whole story, just an epilogue . . . unlike you and me, who had years and years to remember together, and to talk about, but now we'll each die alone— *(Stopping suddenly)*

HUGH: Please don't move away. Please. I want . . . I *need* you here.

LINDY: For what? Say it, Hugh. For sex.

HUGH: With you it's more . . . *(He approaches awkwardly and kisses her)* Would it be strange if we made love?

LINDY: Then I'd show you out the door till next time? Adam and I used to lie for hours afterwards, talking face to face while he was still inside me. He could make his thing twitch—

HUGH: Stop it, Lindy.

LINDY: Your Lena turns me on, I admit it. Why not ask her to join us for breakfast. Isn't politics about getting in bed with the enemy? *(Beat)* I'm teasing, Jesus.

HUGH *(After a moment)*: I'd like to make love to you.

LINDY: See how liberating it is to speak the truth?

HUGH: May I?

LINDY: But this'll be on my terms.

HUGH: You're negotiating?

LINDY: Things blew apart so fast I had no time to lawyer-up. Now you come here wanting more, you shameless motherfucker. And it's a seller's market.

HUGH (*Almost smug*): I'm listening.

LINDY (*Thinks*): Five hundred dollars. (*He snorts a laugh*) You're right, why undervalue the goodies; make it a thousand. I'll sleep with you for one thousand dollars.

HUGH (*Stung, furious, confused*): You're a genius, Lindy . . . you know every move with me, and when I'm vulnerable you pull the rug out: "It was the crazies talking, you didn't take me seriously, did you?"

LINDY: It's the "serious" talking. One thousand.

HUGH (*Trying not to fall for it*): May I bring some tea . . . and a danish?

LINDY: It's all included at Lindy's Boink and Breakfast. But if you leave now, the next time you come by, it'll be two thousand, and four the time after. With each refusal, the price doubles.

HUGH: You're sick.

LINDY: Well, duh, Hubert. Going once. Going twice—

HUGH: Fine.

LINDY: Fine . . . *what?*

HUGH: I'll pay.

LINDY: You'll pay what? For what?

HUGH: Five hundred dollars. For sex with you.

LINDY: *"Five hundred."* (*With a smile*) I might have weakened if you'd been straight with me, but even now, when you come a-beggin', you try and lowball me.

HUGH: Fine. One thousand.

LINDY: Go get some cash. You know where to find me: House of the Outlaw Sprinklers.

HUGH *(Beat)*: Banks aren't open yet.

LINDY: Get a ten-percent deposit from the ATM at the mall. One hundred. And, yes, I'd love Earl Grey.

HUGH *(Beat)*: You need more money, is that it? I'll have Steubenhauer adjust the agreement. He'll find someone to pay twice market value for the house, anything, just tell me what, what the fuck you want—

LINDY: Too late.

HUGH *(Starts to leave, then turns back, an appeal)*: Lindy—

LINDY: We'll all attend all your weddings, me and the kids, smiling. Fuck me, Hugh, then go home to your condo and sleep alone with whoever's camping out in your life. I'll do the same.

HUGH: Good-bye, Lindy.

(He starts out.)

LINDY: What a waste. *(He stops)* This might have all been— what's it called, that last flare-up before the fires die? I had mine. You had yours. A little more patience and maybe we'd have— We're both difficult, you know. But you were better around me, for a time. And I felt safe with you, for a time. Good-bye, Little Country. Boom!

(They are both still. Then Hugh leaves.
  A cell phone rings. Lindy is momentarily disoriented.)
  The ringing stops. She waves it away and resumes mixing paint. The cell phone rings again. She looks around and finds her phone.
  She reads the display. She speaks with calm finality:)

No, Adam. It's over.

(She ends the call, then turns up the music louder. Then she takes the paint to the wall and starts painting.
    A moment passes.
    The lights dim.)

END OF PLAY

Sooner or later any playwright—perhaps any writer—who agrees to talk in public about his work will be asked the dread question: "Where do you get your ideas?" It's a curiosity both generous and naive: generous for showing an interest in what we writers do; and naive because it assumes that we have any idea where it all comes from.

As a rule, by the time a play has wriggled out of the embryonic "idea" phase, and been exposed to the elements, revised, undergone invasive procedures, fed, exercised, transformed—namely, after the years it often takes for the animal to stand up and walk on its two hind legs—an author has lost all memory of the "idea" that gave it birth.

But in some cases we *do* remember. This trilogy is a case in point. In the hope that it might serve as a partial answer to where *one* writer's idea came from, and how it evolved, I offer this retrospective.

First, the raw material. Years ago while rehearsing an early play of mine, I became aware of a young woman (an assistant stage manager fresh out of college) who was pursued by all the available young men in the company. She wasn't notably attractive—more *wholesome*—but she had a sleepy sensuality, a ready chuckle, and an easygoing manner that made her great fun to be around. On several occasions I caught her eye and noticed something like wariness in her expression. I can't remember a thing that passed between her and me except a random exchange one night as a group of us dropped her off after a movie and pizza. It went something like, "What are your plans in theater?" She looked puzzled. I expanded, "You obviously have talent," (everyone agreed that she was a crackerjack stage manager) "and so I was curious about your next step." She looked suddenly furious, as if I'd opened a can of worms, and with a tight smile she said good night, turned away and left us.

In the following years she came to mind no more or less than any number of engaging acquaintances, but when she did, it was that odd exchange, that sudden flash of anger, that came to mind first. And then, maybe fifteen years later, just before I was to give a talk in the Midwest, she left a phone message to say that she had heard I was speaking at such and such a place, which was very close to where she lived. She wanted to attend my presentation, but hoped I wouldn't think her rude if she dashed away immediately afterward, since she had to be home by midnight. I left her a message, no problem, see you there.

The woman who appeared was a poised socialite, dressed with elegant simplicity, her manner charming and polished, not a trace of the girl-next-door quality I remembered. It was a pity we wouldn't have more time to catch up. I was intrigued by the change in her, and made a note to myself that at some point when time allowed I'd be in touch with her to learn more about her surprising transformation.

At the reception following my talk, I saw her mingling easily with the rather high-end arts-foundation crowd. I was able to gather that her husband was a man of some consequence in the state. As the evening broke up, she asked if I had time for a drink. Since it was nearly eleven o'clock, I asked her how long her drive home was. She said not to worry about it. She knew of a private club that served after hours. Suddenly the situation took on a different hue.

We spent the next three hours drinking wine and talking. That is, *she* talked, and I asked occasional questions. Mostly I sat dumbfounded, not so much because of any specific events she narrated (married upwards, husband locally connected, remade her life for him, gave up art, had children, ran a home, tried to keep the embers of creativity aglow by stage-managing local amateur theatricals, etc., etc.); it was more her measured but feverish urgency, the compulsion of her thoughts, her need to talk, and by the manner of her speech: sudden bursts of revelation followed by long silences, like an athlete rallying for the next round. I was completely submersed in the rhythm of her life, and for the time we spent together I lost all sense of myself.

At one point I asked if she remembered the exchange we'd had after the film and pizza. And before the thought was half out, she shot back a *yes*, as if she'd been waiting for the question. She went on to explain her medical condition, a thing that had colored every decision in her life. It was a source of torment to her ever since she was diagnosed as a teenager . . . hence her abrupt change of mood that night when I asked about her future plans. The exact details of her story are, of course, a private matter (though a few, heavily disguised, have found their way into the trilogy), but what struck me as she said good night and drove away (at two A.M.), was that I had just had an evening with a woman that felt far more erotic and sexual than an act of physical love.

I felt I had *experienced* her life—*inhabited* it. This was a new and surprising sensation, and it held a mystery I couldn't quite grasp: how the intense intimacy, the *eros* inherent in a person *verbally* opening themselves to another could feel more sensual than making love with them. None of this presented itself as an "idea" for a play. As life goes, the encounter was more a puzzle to work out in my own mind, something to do with the paradoxical nature of human interchange; that we can *make love* with little connection to our partner, but then talk to someone in a way that feels closer than sex.

Now to the trilogy. It began with a failure. The initial "plan" was to write a play in "real continuous time." My challenge would be that what happened on stage between "lights up" and "curtain" would have to occur in exactly the time it would take in real life. All the events, the surprises, the turns, would have to happen plausibly in, say, two hours of unbroken time.

Next, I intended to limit the cast to two. Why two? There were several reasons. For most of my early career I wrote plays with large casts. I'd learned my stage chops in the UK, where I'd gone for a year of graduate study under the remarkable Stephen Joseph at Manchester University. I stayed on in London for seven more years. At the time, British rep companies regularly mounted large-cast plays, so this is what I grew to like and admire. Such plays helped keep a large company of players seasonally employed, and happy. These plays were also a natural outgrowth of a theater culture in which playwrights tried to draw portraits of a whole society—the more characters one could put on stage, the more complete the portrait. I brought this habit back with me to America, when I returned to live here in 1972. But I found, to my alarm, that as American theater became financially beleaguered, the first victims were actors. Casts shrank and, gradually, so did the frequency of my productions.

A two-character play was, in part, a practical matter, a way to survive, to enhance my chance of production. But there was something else at work. I was becoming interested in questions of dramatic economy. What might be minimally required to keep a situation interesting on stage. Could one manage it in real continuous time with only two actors? Could one design a series of events with sufficient variety, surprise and emotional interest to keep an audience engaged?

In college I was a composer. Like most composition students, for a period, I fell under the spell of Bach's Two Part Inventions. The variety of texture and movement that Bach achieved with just two melodic lines seemed to me a pinnacle of condensed emotive and structural thinking, and I wanted to one day attempt such concision—perhaps in the form of an extended piece for piano with only two melodic lines. For various reasons, I stopped composing. But the dream of writing for two "voices" seems to have resurfaced in a new form—*two characters.*

What would such a play be about? Following Aristotle's shrewd observation that families are good subjects for drama because we all (most of us) have one, and therefore recognize feelingly the behavior they display in crisis, I reasoned that two people, a man and a woman, trying to connect in some deep way, might make a good starting point. Everyone longs to connect with another soul. So who would this man and woman be, their situation?

If they were meeting for the first time, I (and they) would be hobbled by a lack of shared experience, something that could be understood and identified with by an audience. So I decided that my couple would have a friendship from years before . . . Maybe an *intimate* one?

Only then did the lightbulb go on—yes, I am that stupid. You see, it's not about *where* ideas come from. They're everywhere, all the time. It's more a question of *noticing* them—an act of acute *attention*—that "eureka" moment people talk about, the moment of *inspiration.*

I began speculating about my meeting with—call her Melinda (which is what I *did* finally name her for these plays). What if a man like me, and a woman like her, had known each other earlier under some circumstances and their liaison ended abruptly, without resolution? What if years later, they had met again to catch up, both married with families, both confident that the past was buried. But as the night wore on, things began to veer toward feelings (both sexual and emotional) that turned up the heat under the cool self-presentation, until finally they were forced to confront fault lines in their current lives? How would such an encounter unfold? Among other things, such a setup would allow me to explore the notion of sex versus *talk* as a gateway to intimacy.

This seemed promising. I began to write. After several weeks, fifteen pages into the work, I felt a chill. Something wasn't right. I put the pages away and got on with other work, but the challenge of the play remained a constant irritant. One day I picked up the opening scene and started writing again. Ten more pages quickly followed. I was excited. Things were flowing again. Perhaps I'd initially misjudged what I had. I sat back and read it again. It was *terrible*. Boring, aimless yammer about nothing.

How was I going to keep this thing going in continuous real time for two hours when I already put myself to sleep in the first fifteen minutes? I was in a sweat. I'd been planning to write this work for ten years. It was now a personal challenge. I had deliberately cleared a slot in my schedule to tackle it. And—nothing!

I threw out the original pages and began fresh, writing in a fury, in the hope that with a vigorous enough warm-up, like the cartoon character who starts a chase with legs churning into a blurred circle, I'd achieve momentum enough for the long-distance marathon of writing a full-length play. I finished an initial sprint of maybe twenty pages. The situation on stage had developed to where sexual intimacy looked like the only possible next step between my two characters. I set the pages aside with a plan to reread them after a break of a few days. From there I'd decide where, if anywhere, to take the story.

According to plan, I returned to work, and read over what I had so far. It actually wasn't too terrible. But now my couple was ready to make love. On stage that's a problem. How does one "imitate" such an action in "continuous real time" within the bounds of propriety? It sounds like a ludicrous dilemma in retrospect, but at the time I was stumped. In frustration—in fact, almost as a joke on myself—I wrote, "The lights fade." Sure, give the poor couple a chance to make love while I ransack my brain for a solution.

"The lights fade." This, by the way, was not a *serious* stage direction. It was me whistling in the dark, the kind of antic/desperate aside I occasionally jot in the margin of a manuscript: "This sucks, make better," or, "Is dentistry still an option?" or, even on rare occasions, "Yes! More!"

"The lights fade."

The object of the exercise, remember, was to see if I could write a play in continuous time. But as I went to sleep that night (I have the notebook entry in front of me), I wrote: "Try *making use* of the breaks, fuck real time." And—knowing me, though this part I don't remember—I probably lay thrashing around for half the night working out how I might use the breaks between scenes as a dramatic opportunity. In other words, I weighed the merits of throwing out my original plan entirely. The more I pondered the idea, the more it intrigued me. What if I *used* scene breaks in an unexpected way—something on the order of Noël Coward's lovely one act *Still Life*—and advanced my story through a series of unanticipated intervening events.

This proved to be a turning point—the notion that I might lead the action to a point where the next event seems inevitable, then after a blackout, bring the lights back up on a situation that had changed in the darkness, so things resumed in a way that was slightly puzzling, mysterious, unexpected.

In the few moments I had while the audience tried to piece together what they'd missed, there would be time to weave in more about my characters' lives and illuminate not just how and why the change had come about during the blackout, but add shade and nuance that would have dragged as part of straightforward exposition. Though this device will strike many writers as simple and obvious, it had an enormous impact on my approach to designing the play, and then on the entire trilogy.

I brought the lights back up with my two characters sitting at opposite sides of a hotel bed, the woman in disarray, breathless, unsettled; and the man confused and frustrated. Gradually we learn what had happened, though we may have already sensed and perhaps feared the volatile nature of their attraction. With this as my new structural principle I wrote with more confidence, freed of the bogeyman of "real continuous time." In fact I had something much better—a way to make my story unexpected without recourse to rigged behavior—just ordinary events that took place behind the audience's back, as it were, and, with luck, intensified its desire to know what it had missed.

This same technique yielded the play's conclusion. If I proceeded with scene ends that slightly destabilized an audience's expectation, the end of the play itself could be made "uncertain." We'd have closure, but wouldn't be able to decide how the future might go between the two people left alone on stage as the lights dimmed to black.

With this, I had my play *Do Not Disturb*.

But this volume is a trilogy. How did the other two plays come about?

Do Not Disturb was performed in London in 2002, starring two superb actors: Gillian Anderson (fresh from ten years tracking mischievous aliens on TV's *X-Files*), and the estimable Roger Allam. A consistent response to the play was that when the two characters talked about their respective marriages there was no way to tell if they were speaking the truth, or angling the lighting to make the merchandise sparkle.

Interesting. I myself began to wonder how honest they were. By the end of the play both were on the verge of leaving their respective marriages and running off to pursue a last chance for happiness. But was this near-plan a delusion? Would they do it? Did they? Should they? Something about the end of the play seemed to open as many doors as it closed.

What if I wrote a "companion play" about the married life of each couple, perhaps scenes alternating back and forth between them. But that seemed mechanical, and it felt like a violation of my discipline: two voices. Two-plus-two was a cop-out. But . . . what if I wrote *two more plays*, each treating one of the marriages. I could explore their lives from an entirely new perspective, and create a triangulation from which an audience might better judge them in the first play.

This was scary. I consider myself lucky (and challenged) enough when I come up with a notion for just *one play*. But *two*? Two whole new plays? Still, there was something appealing in the idea that I might view my first play as a found object, a piece written by another writer, and my job would be to expand on each of the characters by showing them in a marriage about which I could assume nothing beyond what that first playwright had told me.

Over my desk I have a card that reads: "The first draft is by someone else," a reminder that however badly a piece might be going, no one has to see it. Once the first draft is done, I'm no longer alone at my desk. The job is now between me, The First Draft, and the piece I really want to write. In the case of *Do Not Disturb*, I could pretend to be paying tribute, expanding on a play by someone else who had simply neglected to tell us all we wanted to know.

I decided to continue the structural principle that had helped me "discover" the first play, leading the audience to moments where the next action is fairly predictable, then resuming with a situation that had shifted. Each of the two new plays would be for two characters in a marriage; three interlocking two-part inventions, as it were.

The second play, *Fifty Words*, though it took two more years before the writing began, went on the page relatively fast. The two critical decisions to be made were the time span of the action, and *when* it took place relative to the actions of the first play. I quickly hit on a single night as the time frame, but should I write about the marriage up until the point in the first play when the husband, Adam, sets off to meet Melinda, his lover from a decade before? This might be effective for people who knew what lay ahead, and the rumble of doom as he left his house would mean something to those in the know. But I decided when I undertook the second play that each work had to be stand-alone. Which meant that any link between them would not depend on an audience having seen a play other than it was now watching. I decided to "hinge" the first two plays on a phone call involving Adam's mistress, Melinda. I'll say no more than that. In terms of play two (*Fifty Words*), we wouldn't have to know a thing about the person behind the call, except that she was "the other woman." Those who knew *Do Not Disturb* would have a more nuanced experience of who had set things in motion in *Fifty Words*, but those seeing *Fifty Words* by itself wouldn't be left out.

Once this "common joint" was determined, I needed an element to make the situation between the husband and wife emotionally raw, a circumstance in itself out of the ordinary, but one that wasn't contrived or artificial. I hit on the idea of their nine-year-old son being away on a sleepover, his first ever. It felt to me as if, without another word, this fact suggested several loaded issues in the marriage: that these were extremely caring parents, and/or the child might be emotionally fragile. Once these facts were in place, the action laid itself out smoothly. Until the final scene, that is.

I discovered that this second play was a more intense business than the first. It built to a crisis that demanded a showdown more raw and volatile than all that went before. This kind of job-order pressure is never good to bring with you to the toolshed, but I felt the play would stand or fall in performance according to how plausible and fresh I could make this final scene. The answer came on a flight from Long Beach to New York. Two women behind me were in a heated (well, *loud,* anyway) discussion regarding the generally deplorable species "Modern Husband," and one of them, who had recently been abandoned by the fauna in question, let fly with: "You know what I wanted to do when I found out, I wanted to force him to give me her phone number . . ." And before she finished, the other one blurted: "Oh god, me, too, that's exactly what I've always thought I'd do." And what they wanted to do became my final action in *Fifty Words*, stolen from two innocent (but loud) passengers aboard JetBlue.

Where do ideas come from? . . .

Fifty Words was staged a mere six years after completion, and it began my valued association with Manhattan Class Company. Its cast was stunning (Elizabeth Marvel and Norbert Leo Butz), and the director, Austin Pendleton, delivered a magical, seamless, atmospherically astute production. (Austin, by the way, is the most brilliant all-around theatrical mind I know, a treasure trove of every theatrical discipline: performance, writing, aesthetics, history, anecdote, etc. It would be a great disservice to the last five decades of our stage if no one makes a living archive of his life.)

Side Effects, play three, was begun a year before *Fifty Words* premiered and was in its way the trickiest of the trilogy to create. The action of the first two plays each spanned a single night, but I felt that this final drama had to cover a longer period of time. I wanted the audience to see the central character (Melinda, from the first play) as a functioning housewife, mother and career woman, before showing, in graphic terms, the medical issue that haunted her existence. I also wanted her to be heroic and sympathetic, although what she was doing throughout most of the play was far from praiseworthy.

The other critical component was *when* this play took place in relationship to the first two. I decided that, at the start of the play, the wife, Melinda, should not yet have "resumed" her past affair with Adam. It felt stronger to introduce her on the night she first heard from her long-ago lover after a ten-year silence. Her mysterious disappearance from a dinner party hours prior to the first scene could be mistaken for many things that her husband would have reason to worry about, and only when we had some grasp of their life as a couple would I let the audience know what was truly behind her flight. We would then share her secret, and wait for her husband to discover it.

But also, I wanted to see if I could develop and extend my technique of subtly "misleading" with scene breaks that undermine expectation. Given the span of a year, I couldn't bring the couple back into the action "later that night." It had to be *later that year*, and so the surprises had to be of a somewhat different order, a more extreme way of playing with an audience's perspective: "Oh, it's *that* kind of marriage . . ." Followed by a scene that made them reassess their judgment: "But I thought they were . . ." Only to find that ensuing scenes presented a couple moving through far more treacherous and complex interdependency than we at first suspected.

With these decisions in place, the writing moved ahead smoothly. The great surprise with *Side Effects* was how *my own perspective* on it continually changed. And changed again. The moment I finished a draft, the world of the action would start to feel different to me. A new element of the relationship would emerge as central, and I'd have to rethink the play *in new colors*, if you will. More than the other two plays, this one teased me, shifted shape, showed itself in a new light with each revision (eleven and counting). Somehow, my decision to play with the audience's perspective finally had an equally disorienting effect on my own.

Looking back, the absorbing pleasure in working on this trilogy has been the discovery and elaboration of a technique almost geometrically opposite my initial plan. The failure of my original idea to write in continuous time forced me to think about what audiences know and don't know as a play unfolds, and to experiment with the placement and manipulation of events unseen by them. The tension between the seen and the unseen has absorbed my attention throughout my many years of writing these plays.

And, finally, with this volume, I have a completed set of interlocking plays in a beautiful edition published by TCG. My dream, of course, is that some intrepid theater will see its way to mounting all three in successive seasons (or even in one?!). I'd love to see the effect of this mosaic narrative told in a span of time when the previous perspective is fresh in an audience's mind as it watches the next play unfold. This publication will, I hope, be the perfect invitation.

Michael Weller
Brooklyn, New York
April 2011

Michael Weller studied music composition at Brandeis University with Irving Fine, Harold Shapero and Martin Boykan, then worked as a jazz pianist before taking his graduate degree in theater at the University of Manchester, England.

His best known plays are *Moonchildren*, *Fishing*, *Loose Ends*, *Spoils of War* and *Fifty Words*. He has written the screenplays for *Hair* and *Ragtime* (Milos Forman, director), *Lost Angels* (Hugh Hudson, director) and the teleplay of his Broadway drama *Spoils of War*, starring Kate Nelligan. He recently wrote the book for the musical adaptation of *Doctor Zhivago* (Des McAnuff, director; Lucy Simon, music).

His work has received an Academy Award nomination, a NAACP Outstanding Contribution Award, an Outer Critics Circle Award, a Rockefeller Foundation Grant, a Kennedy Center Fund for New American Plays Award, a Helen Merrill Playwriting Award and a Flora Roberts Award. He was honored by The Broken Watch Theatre Company, which gave its playhouse his name.

He designed and co-founded the Mentor Project of the Cherry Lane Theatre, and served for ten years as its supervising mentor. He is president of the Foundation of the Writers Guild of America, East, and serves on the council of The Dramatists Guild of America.